THE INCREDIBLE CHICAGO CUBS TRIVIA BOOK

THE INCREDIBLE CHICAGO CUBS TRIVIA BOOK

300 QUESTIONS FOR THE SUPER-FAN

AL YELLON

Sports Publishing books may be purchased in bulk at special discounts for sales promotion, corporate gifts, fund-raising, or educational purposes. Special editions can also be created to specifications. For details, contact the Special Sales Department, Sports Publishing, 307 Fifth Avenue, 4th Floor, New York, NY 10016 or sportspubbooks@skyhorsepublishing.com.

Sports Publishing® is a registered trademark of Skyhorse Publishing, Inc.®, a Delaware corporation.

Visit our website at www.sportspubbooks.com.

10 9 8 7 6 5 4 3 2 1

Library of Congress Cataloging-in-Publication Data is available on file.

Cover design by David Ter-Avaneysan
Cover photos credit: Getty Images

Print ISBN: 978-1-68358-527-5
Ebook ISBN: 978-1-68358-528-2

Printed in the United States of America

This book is for every Cubs fan who looked around Wrigley Field and thought, "I wonder when that game I remember happened?" . . . and for every Cubs fan who wondered which player accomplished a feat they remember from some year in the 1970s . . . and for every Cubs fan who watched a game on TV or listened on the radio and couldn't remember what years they heard which men broadcast a memorable game.

In other words . . . for every Cubs fan!

Contents

TEAM HISTORY

QUESTIONS

1. What is the Cubs' unique status among all North American professional sports teams?
   Answer on page 19.

2. What year was the Cubs franchise founded?
   Answer on page 19.

3. What team was it founded specifically to defeat?
   Answer on page 19.

4. Did it do so?
   Answer on page 20.

5. In what organization did the Cubs compete before the formation of the National League?
   Answer on page 20.

6. When and where did the Cubs make their National League debut?
   Answer on page 20.

7. Which of these nicknames did newspapers use to describe the team before they became the Cubs? The Black Stockings, Broncos, Colts, Cowboys, Giant Killers, Microbes, Orphans, Remnants, Spuds, White Stockings, or Zephyrs?
Answer on page 20.

8. Which of these were the nicknames of now-defunct National League opponents? Bisons, Blues, Brown Stockings, Colonels, Cowboys Dark Blues, Hoosiers, Maroons, Mutuals, Ruby Legs, Spiders, Stars, Statesmen, Trojans, or Wolverines?
Answer on page 21.

9. Where in California did the Cubs hold spring training for many years?
Answer on page 21.

10. Where did they hold spring training during World War II?
Answer on page 21.

11. How many National League pennants have the Cubs won? How many teams have won more?
Answer on page 22.

12. The Cubs have played the most regular-season games of any major-league team. Which opponent have they played most often?
Answer on page 22.

13. The Cubs have used the most players, 2,277, of any team. Who was their 1,000th? Who was their 2,000th?
Answer on page 22.

14. What was significant about the Cubs' victory on June 14, 1947?
Answer on page 23.

15. What were the most runs scored by the Cubs in a game?
Answer on page 23.

16. What were the most runs scored in a game by the Cubs in the Modern Era?
Answer on page 23.

17. What were the most runs scored by the Cubs in an inning?
Answer on page 23.

18. What were the most runs scored in an inning by the Cubs in the Modern Era?
Answer on page 23.

19. Under which team ownership have the Cubs made the most postseason appearances?
Answer on page 24.

20. Which early pitcher-manager of the Cubs started a prominent sporting goods company?
Answer on page 24.

21. An early owner of the Cubs made his fortune in the restaurant business. Who was he and what was his nickname?
Answer on page 24.

22. Another early owner was the brother of a United States president. Who was he?
Answer on page 25.

23. In 1891, as the Colts, the team played an unusual home schedule. What was unusual about it?
Answer on page 25.

24. What the first season in which the National League had 12 teams?
Answer on page 25.

25. When did the Cubs play their first home game on a Sunday?
Answer on page 25.

26. What was unusual about the Cubs' schedule in 1896?
Answer on page 25.

27. For many years, the Cubs and Pirates played single games on Sunday in Chicago, sometimes in the middle of a series at Pittsburgh. Why?
Answer on page 26.

28. The Cubs played their final game in 1918 on Labor Day. Why did the season end so early?
Answer on page 26.

29. The Cubs lost the 1918 World Series to the Red Sox in six games. What was unique about the series?
Answer on page 26.

30. When did the Cubs first travel to a series by airplane?
Answer on page 26.

31. What distinction do the Cubs have among National League Central Division teams?
Answer on page 27.

32. The Cubs have played only two games on the final day of a season to decide a title. What were the seasons?
Answer on page 27.

33. What was unique about the first of the two final-day games? What was the outcome?
Answer on page 27.

34. What was unique about the second of the two final-day games? What was the outcome?
Answer on page 27.

35. The Cubs played one other extra game to break a tie for a wild-card berth in the postseason. When was it played?
Answer on page 27.

36. What record did the Cubs establish in 1906?
Answer on page 27.

37. What record did the Cubs establish in 1906–10?
Answer on page 28.

38. Which American League team did the Cubs play first when interleague games began in 1997?
Answer on page 28.

39. Where did the Cubs play their first interleague game outside Chicago?
Answer on page 28.

40. The Cubs played the Royals at Kansas City for the first time in 1998. They had played 10 National League games at Kansas City before the Modern Era. Who were their opponents in those games?
Answer on page 28.

41. The Cubs have played one regular-season game in Iowa. Who was their opponent?
Answer on page 28.

42. How many games have the Cubs played outside North America? Where were they played and who were their opponents?
Answer on page 28.

43. The Cubs have played regular-season games against the Dodgers in ballparks in three states. What were the states?
Answer on page 28.

44. Which Cub played the National Anthem before a game on his trumpet?
Answer on page 28.

45. Which Cub employed self-hypnosis and talked to the ball?
Answer on page 28.

46. Which Cub signed a blank contract because he so greatly wanted to play at Wrigley Field?
Answer on page 28.

47. Eleven different Cubs have been recognized as the National League's Most Valuable Player. Name as many as you can.
Answer on page 28.

48. Five Cubs pitchers have won the Cy Young Award. Name them.
Answer on page 29.

49. Six Cubs have been honored as Rookie of the Year. Name them.
Answer on page 29.

50. Thirty-five players have played for the Cubs before turning 20 years old, including 24 since 1901, first season of the Modern Era. Who was the youngest, at 17 years and 300 days?
Answer on page 29.

51. Who was the youngest pitcher as a Cub?
Answer on page 29.

52. Only one of the 35 teenage Cubs played more than 49 games for the team before turning 20. Who was the one?
Answer on page 29.

53. Who was the oldest player to appear in a game as a Cub?
Answer on page 29.

54. Cap Anson played 146 games in 1892, when he turned 40. He played at least 100 in four of his five later seasons. Name the only Cub in the Modern Era who played 100 or more games in his age-40 season.
Answer on page 29.

55. Three other Cubs played at least 50 games in their age-40 or higher season. Name them.
Answer on page 30.

56. Two Cubs pitchers appeared in at least 40 games of a season in which they turned 40 or older. Who were they?
Answer on page 30.

57. Here are the nicknames of some Cubs. Identify the players to which they belonged:

Animalistic

1. Bull	A. Dave Kingman
2. Crab	B. Guy Bush
3. Hawk	C. Johnny Evers
4. Kong	D. Lon Warneke
5. Penguin	E. Kyle Schwarber
6. The Arkansas Hummingbird	F. Andre Dawson
7. The Mississippi Mudcat	G. Leon Durham
8. Warbird	H. Roy Cey

One-Name Wonders

(Note that one nickname applies to two different players!)

1. Bonehead	A. Milt Pappas
2. Chinski	B. Steve Trout
3. Gimpy	C. Fred Merkle
4. Honker	D. Kris Bryant
5. Husk	E. Phil Cavarretta
6. Philliabuck	F. Johnny Evers
7. Rainbow	G. Randy Hundley
8. Rebel	H. Charlie Root
9. Sarge	I. Frank Schulte
10. Sparkles	J. Frank Chance
11. Swish	K. Gary Matthews
12. Trojan	L. Hank Sauer
13. Wildlife	M. Steve Swisher
14. Zonk	N. Keith Moreland
	O. Bill Nicholson

Leadership

(Note that one nickname applies to two different players!)

1. Big Daddy	A. Frank Chance
2. Mr. Cub	B. Rick Reuschel
3. The Peerless Leader	C. Greg Maddux
4. The Polish Prince	D. Mike Krukow
5. The Professor	E. Rick Sutcliffe
6. The Red Baron	F. Kyle Hendricks
	G. Ernie Banks

Other Dandies

1. Big Z	A. Javier Baez
2. Dandy Little Glove Man	B. Billy Williams
3. El Mago	C. Carlos Zambrano
4. Jolly Cholly	D. Charlie Grimm
5. Old Tomato Face	E. Cap Anson
6. Sweet Swinger	F. Gabby Hartnett
7. The Marshalltown Infant	G. Mickey Morandini

Answers on page 30.

58. What was the name of the Cubs' first National League home park?
Answer on page 30.

59. In 1884, the Cubs, then the White Stockings, hit 142 home runs, 103 more than any other team. Why?
Answer on page 30.

60. Which Cub hit 27 home runs in 1884, a record that stood until Babe Ruth hit 29 in 1919?
Answer on page 31.

61. Why were the Cubs forced to leave Lakefront Park after 1884?
Answer on page 31.

62. Wrigley Field is the Cubs' second home ballpark that was built for another team. What was the first?
Answer on page 31.

63. Who was the Cubs' on-field announcer of starting lineups, pinch hitters, and changes of pitchers and players in the field from 1916–74?
Answer on page 31.

64. What was his famous announcement before each game?
Answer on page 31.

65. On September 17, 1953, Ernie Banks became the Cubs' first Black player to appear in a game. Another Black player actually signed with the Cubs before Banks, on September 1, but did not appear in a game until September 20. Who was he?
Answer on page 32.

66. Ernie Banks was the Cubs' shortstop from his arrival in 1953 through May 21, 1961, when his ailing knees prompted him to change positions. What was his new position?
Answer on page 32.

WARNING! OBSCURE PLAYERS ALERT!

67. Who hit the Cubs' first National League home run?
Answer on page 32.

68. Who hit the Cubs' first National League home run at home?
Answer on page 33.

69. Who hit the Cubs' first home run at their current home park?
Answer on page 33.

70. Which Cubs star outfielder before the Modern Era retired because his fiancée's father would not allow her to marry a baseball player?
Answer on page 33.

71. One of the most famous of all baseball trivia questions: Who was the third baseman when the Cubs had their famous double-play combination of shortstop Joe Tinker, second baseman Johnny Evers, and first baseman Frank Chance?
Answer on page 33.

72. Who was the usual catcher when Tinker, Evers, and Chance were in the infield?
Answer on page 34.

73. Who were the usual starting outfielders in those glory years?
Answer on page 34.

74. When were Tinker, Evers, and Chance elected to the Hall of Fame?
Answer on page 34.

75. Tinker, Evers, and Chance were immortalized in the eight-line poem, "Baseball's Sad Lexicon," published in the *New York Evening Mail* on July 12, 1910. Recite the poem.
Answer on page 34.

76. What is a "gonfalon?"
Answer on page 34.

77. How many double plays did the Cubs make that went from Tinker to Evers to Chance?
Answer on page 35.

78. Seven of the twenty-four players who earned the highest WAR as Cubs came to the team in trades. What team did each come from, when, and what did the Cubs exchange for them?
Answer on page 35.

79. Fifteen of the thirty-two men who played at least 1,000 games as a Cub were traded to other teams. What team was each dealt to and when?
Answer on page 36.

80. From 1903 through 1942, in most seasons when they did not win the pennant, what did the Cubs do after the end of the National League season?
Answer on page 37.

81. The Cubs played many exhibition games in their long history from which the proceeds went to various causes, including 23 Boys' Benefit games in 1949–72, and games for Canadian war relief in 1917, for unemployment relief in 1931 and for US war relief in 1945. On September 28, 1905, they played a regular-season game at home against Boston, with all revenue going to one person. Who was the person?
Answer on page 37.

82. What did the Cubs, then known as the White Stockings, do after the 1888 season?
Answer on page 37.

83. In 1913, the Cubs were the first big league team to train on the west coast of Florida. In what city did they train?
Answer on page 38.

84. A sportswriter called the Cubs "the Grimm Gypsies" in 1936. Why?
Answer on page 38.

85. The Cubs have held spring training in cities in nine states. Name as many of the states as you can.
Answer on page 38.

86. The Cubs have trained in Mesa, Arizona, since 1979. They also trained in Mesa from 1952–65. In what other Arizona city did they train, from 1967–78?
Answer on page 38.

87. During the Modern Era, the Cubs have played 244 exhibition games during the regular season. They lost five of seven games against one opponent. Who was the opponent?
Answer on page 39.

88. When did the Cubs play their last in-season exhibition game against a major-league opponent?
Answer on page 39.

89. When did the Cubs play their last in-season exhibition game against any opponent?
Answer on page 39.

ONE AND DONE

Since 1901, the first season of the Modern Era, the Cubs have won 258 regular-season games by a score of 1–0. They have lost 259.

90. Which Cub drove in the game's only run most often?
Answer on page 39.

91. In how many of the wins did their only run come on a home run?
Answer on page 39.

92. Which two Cubs homered for the only run in three games each?
Answer on page 39.

93. Name the four Cubs who had homers in 1–0 games two different times and no other plays that produced the only run of a game.
Answer on page 39.

94. Who was the only Cubs pitcher to homer in a 1–0 win?
Answer on page 39.

95. The most common run-scoring play in a 1–0 win was a single, 73 times. A home run was second. What two plays were tied for third, 23 times?
Answer on page 40

96. The Cubs have won, 1–0, on one type of play once. What was the play?
Answer on page 40.

97. How many of the 1–0 wins were walk-offs?
Answer on page 40.

98. How many of the 1–0 wins were walk-offs on home runs?
Answer on page 40.

WALK THE WALK

99. Since 1876, first year of the National League, how many regular-season games have the Cubs won on walk-offs?
Answer on page 40.

100. How many walk-off wins have they had at Wrigley Field?
Answer on page 40.

101. The Cubs have had walk-off wins against 35 different teams. Which team have they walked off most often?
Answer on page 40.

102. A total of 419 different Cubs have been the last batter in a walk-off win. Who did it most often?
Answer on page 41.

103. Were more of the walk-off wins in the ninth inning or extra innings?
Answer on page 41.

104. What were the Cubs' longest walk-off wins by innings?
Answer on page 41.

105. Just over half of all walk-off wins, 500, have come on singles. Home runs are second most common. How many walk-off homers have the Cubs hit?
Answer on page 41.

106. How many of the walk-off wins came on walks?
Answer on page 41.

107. How many came on a batter hit by a pitch?
Answer on page 41.

108. Only one walk-off win came on one type of play. What was it?
Answer on page 41.

TEAM HISTORY

ANSWERS

1. The Cubs are the oldest team still in its original city. A group of Chicago businessmen gathered at a downtown hotel on October 1, 1869, to create a professional baseball team representing the city.

They wanted their team to defeat the Cincinnati Red Stockings, the first professional baseball team, who had handily beaten several of Chicago's best amateur teams when they came to Chicago in 1869.

The new team, the White Stockings, won at Cincinnati on September 7, 1870. The next day's *Chicago Tribune* had no fewer than seven headlines above its account of the game, leading with "The Redoubtable Red Stockings Defeated by Chicago's $18,000 Nine."

2. The White Stockings played in the National Association, the first true league, in 1871 and 1874–75. The team suspended operations after 1871 due to the Great Chicago Fire. Its stockholders actually voted at one point to fold the team and sell off its assets, then changed their mind.

3. The famed Cincinnati Red Stockings, who were the first professional baseball team, founded in 1869.

4. Yes, they did so twice—both times in 1870—first at Cincinnati, then in Chicago. After the season, the Red Stockings disbanded when their top players, George and Harry Wright, signed to play in Boston. The *Chicago Tribune* suggested that the White Stockings should do the same, lest they suffer the same fate the following year.

5. The franchise we now know as the Chicago Cubs began play as the Chicago White Stockings in 1871, in a loosely organized league called the National Association of Base Ball Clubs. They would play just 28 games, going 19–9, and then suspend play until 1874 because of the Great Chicago Fire of October 1871. The fire took a tremendous toll on the city, and it took a while for it to rebuild.

6. The Cubs' very first National League game was played on Tuesday, April 25, 1876, in Louisville, then part of the eight-team league. The Cubs, then known as White Stockings, defeated the Louisville Grays, 4–0. About 2,000 attended and saw pitcher Albert Spalding record three of the Cubs' eight hits, as well as pitch a shutout and allowing seven hits. The team would play its first home game two weeks later, Wednesday, May 10, defeating Cincinnati, also by shutout, 6–0. They could then have been called "South Siders," as their first NL home park was located at 23rd Street near State Street. They would play two seasons there before moving to Lakefront Park, near the current intersection of Randolph and Michigan.

7. All of the listed nicknames were used to refer to what we often heard called "The Chicago National League Ball Club" in its early days. "Cubs" was first used by a newspaper headline writer named Fred A. Hayner, who worked for the *Chicago Daily News*. According to a 2016 *Chicago Sun-Times* article by his grandson Don Hayner, also a sportswriter, Fred first wrote the name *Cubs* to refer to the young players on the Chicago NL team in a *Daily News* article March 27, 1902, a few weeks before the season began.

The article, headlined "Selee Places His Men," mentioned some of the youngsters on the team, which included future Hall of Famers Johnny Evers and Joe Tinker.

Manager Frank Chance liked the name and convinced team ownership to make it the club's official nickname by 1907.

8. All of the listed nicknames were used to refer to various National League opponents in the nineteenth century. In order as listed, the home cities for those teams are: Buffalo (Bisons), Cincinnati and Syracuse (Blues), St. Louis (Brown Stockings), Louisville (Colonels), Kansas City (Cowboys), Hartford (Dark Blues), Indianapolis (Hoosiers), St. Louis again (Maroons), New York (Mutuals), Worcester (Ruby Legs), Cleveland (Spiders), Indianapolis and Cleveland (Stars), Washington (Statesmen), Troy, New York (Trojans) and Detroit (Wolverines).

9. Cubs spring training camps were held at Catalina Island, off the southern California coast, from 1922–51.

The island was owned by William Wrigley, who had bought controlling interest in the Cubs in 1918 and Catalina the following year. For many years it was considered a good location for training camp because of its isolation, so that players could focus on baseball. Over time, though, it became too difficult to play exhibition games against other teams, and the Cubs relocated to Mesa, Arizona, for spring training in 1952.

10. During World War II, travel restrictions were put in place in the United States, so the Cubs and other teams could not travel to their usual spring training locations. Commissioner Albert "Happy" Chandler decreed that MLB teams should train north of the Mason-Dixon line and east of the Mississippi River.

So from 1943–45, Cubs training camp was held at a resort in French Lick, Indiana, a small town about 75 miles west of Louisville. Weather conditions weren't exactly ideal, and at times games were postponed by early-spring snowstorms.

After the war, Cubs training camp returned to Catalina Island through 1951.

11. The Cubs have won 17 National League pennants. Six of these were in the nineteenth century and 11 have come in the World Series era, since 1903. The Dodgers (26 league championships), Giants (23) and Cardinals (19) have more NL titles than the Cubs.

12. Through the end of 2025, the Cubs have faced the St. Louis Cardinals most often, with 2,404 games between the two clubs. The Cubs have won 1,211 and lost 1,176, with 17 ties. That's just two more times than the Cubs have faced the Pirates, 2,402 through the end of the 2025 season. Even with the Pirates' rough last three decades, they still have an all-time lead over the Cubs, 1,220 Pirates wins and 1,171 Cubs wins, with 11 ties.

13. The 1,000th player in Cubs history was a 21-year-old callup who went 0-for-4 in his first game August 6, 1959, in a 4–2 win over the Phillies. At the time, few would have guessed that young player would become one of the most important figures in franchise history: Billy Williams, who played 16 years with the team, hit 394 home runs as a Cub and was elected to the Hall of Fame in 1987.

The 2,000th Cubs player was Clayton Richard, a left-handed swingman who pitched for the Cubs in 2015 and 2016. He made his Cubs debut July 4, 2015, against the Marlins, starting the game against them in Wrigley Field. The Cubs won the game, 7–2, and Richard threw 6 1/3 strong innings, allowing seven hits and two runs.

14. On this day the Cubs defeated the Phillies, 6–3, the last of a five-game winning streak. The victory put the Cubs 1,179 wins above .500, their all-time high. Entering the 2026 season they were 582 games over .500 all-time.

15. The Cubs (then generally referred to as "Colts") scored 36 runs against Louisville on June 29, 1897, at West Side Grounds. They were helped by 10 Louisville errors; just 12 of the Chicago runs were earned. Jimmy Ryan and Barry McCormick led the way with five runs each and the team had 30 hits and 47 total bases, both records at the time. The hit and total base records have been broken, but the 36 runs remains the all-time MLB record for a single game.

16. In the Modern Era, the Cubs record for runs is 26, accomplished against Philadelphia at Wrigley Field, on Aug. 25, 1922. The 49 runs combined is the MLB record for a game of any length. The Cubs matched that 26-run total in a game against the Rockies at Coors Field, defeating Colorado 26–7 on August 18, 1995.

17. The most runs scored in an inning by the Cubs (then generally referred to as "White Stockings") is 18, in the seventh inning vs. Detroit on September 6, 1883, in a game they won 26–6. It was the last of a five-game stretch in which they scored double digits every game and outscored their opponents 86–23. Even so, that team finished second in the National League. The 18 runs is also the all-time MLB record, and also holds the record for batters faced in an inning (23, later tied), and most players scoring three runs in an inning (two, Tommy Burns and Ned Williamson).

18. In the Modern Era, the Cubs record for runs in a single inning is 14, set in the wild 26–23 win over the Phillies August 25, 1922. The 14 runs were scored in the fourth inning, the

Cubs' second double-digit inning of the game (also 10 in the second inning) and gave them a 19-run lead, 25–6. Nevertheless, they had to hang on to win by just three runs, and the Phillies had the bases loaded when the charmingly named Bevo LeBourveau struck out to end the game.

19. Entering the 2026 season, three Cubs ownership groups share the correct answer to this question. The Wrigleys (NL pennants in 1918, 1929, 1932, 1938, and 1945), Tribune Co. (division titles in 1984, 1989, 2003, 2007, and 2008 and a wild-card spot in 1998) and the Ricketts family (wild-card spots in 2015, 2018 and 2025, division titles in 2017 and 2020, and the World Series title in 2016) all have six postseason appearances to their credit. Thus, if the Cubs make the postseason again under the Ricketts ownership, that will be a new record of seven.

20. Albert Spalding pitched for the Chicago NL franchise that's now the Cubs in 1876—in fact, he was their primary pitcher, starting 60 of the 66 games—and also their manager in 1876 and 1877.

But even as he did that, and continued as a part-owner and executive for the team for more than another decade, he and his brother opened a sporting goods store in Chicago. By 1901 he owned 14 such stores and eventually the company turned into what is still the Spalding sporting goods company, which sells equipment for dozens of sports worldwide.

21. Charles Weeghman, nicknamed "Lucky Charlie," made a fortune in the lunch counter business in Chicago. That money eventually allowed him to become the owner of the Chicago franchise in the Federal League. When that league folded, two of its owners were allowed to buy into the National League, and that's how Weeghman became Cubs owner in 1916. Two years later he sold to a group that included William Wrigley.

22. Charles Taft, brother of US President William Howard Taft, was a minority owner in the group headed by Charles Murphy that bought the Cubs in 1905. Murphy sold his shares to Taft in 1914, and two years later, Taft sold out to Charlie Weeghman.

23. The Cubs (then known mainly as "Colts") had two home parks in 1891. They played Monday, Wednesday, and Friday games at West Side Park and Tuesday, Thursday, and Saturday games at South Side Park II, successor to their original home on 23rd Street. Back then, most teams did not play games on Sundays. In 1892, they played exclusively at South Side Park II, before moving to a new park on the West Side, named West Side Grounds, where they would play through 1915.

24. This is a trick question! You might think the answer is 1969, when the NL expanded from 10 to 12 teams, but the correct answer is 1892, when four teams were added from the American Association after its final season: Louisville, Washington, St. Louis, and Baltimore. The new teams finished ninth through 12th in the order listed. The league contracted back to eight teams in 1900, when three of those clubs—Louisville, Washington, and Baltimore—were eliminated, along with Cleveland, who had their infamous Spiders team go 20–134 in 1899.

25. The Cubs' first Sunday game was played in 1893, a 13–12 loss to Cincinnati on May 14. They began playing on Sundays in an effort to attract some of the large number of weekend visitors to the Chicago World's Fair. To some extent that worked, as eight of the nine largest Cubs crowds in 1893 were on Sundays. (The other was on Memorial Day, when the team played a doubleheader.)

26. The entire 132-game season in 1896 consisted of three road trips and two homestands. The first 10 games were on the road, the next 22 at home, then 22 on the road, 46 (!) at home from June 21–August 13, and the final 32 on the road, from August 14–September 20.

27. Professional baseball was prohibited by law in Pennsylvania on Sunday until 1934. So the teams would hop on a train after their Saturday game, head to Chicago, play there on Sunday, then sometimes go back to Pittsburgh for another game. Back then, series often "wrapped around" a weekend. Though Sunday baseball was legalized in Pennsylvania in 1934, there was still a curfew of 6 p.m. local time there for baseball, so several dozen games at Philadelphia and Pittsburgh, including three involving the Cubs, were suspended and completed later, until that law was repealed in 1960.

28. The federal government ordered baseball to shut down because of World War I. The season thus ended on September 2 and the Cubs were declared NL champions with an 84–45 record, 10 1/2 games ahead of the second-place Giants. They then lost the World Series to the Red Sox four games to two.

29. Due to the ramp-up of World War I, the 1918 World Series was played on six consecutive days, the first three in Chicago, at Comiskey Park, and the next three in Boston, at Fenway Park. Neither team scored more than three runs in any of the games.

The Cubs' home games were played at the White Sox' home stadium because at the time, Weeghman Park held only 14,000 and Comiskey Park's capacity was 28,000. The teams only came close to that capacity once, for Game Three, which drew 27,054.

30. The Cubs first flew to a game Thursday, May 24, 1946, after two games at Brooklyn May 22 and 23. They flew from Newark, New Jersey, to Pittsburgh, site of their next series. A nationwide railroad strike had begun on the afternoon of May 22, prompting the Cubs' flight. They lost both games to the Pirates and had planned to fly from Pittsburgh to Chicago, but heavy fog prevented them from doing so. Instead, they took an overnight train.

31. They are the only NL Central team that began in the National League. The Cardinals, Pirates and Reds started in the American Association. The Brewers started in the American League.

32. The seasons were 1908 and 2018. In 1908, the Giants and Cubs were tied with one game left, so they played that game for the NL pennant. The second was a tiebreaker game for the NL Central title between the Brewers and Cubs. The first was for the pennant; the second, for first place in the division. With MLB postseason spots now determined by standings tie-breakers, that 2018 game, and a Dodgers-Rockies tiebreaker game that same day, will forever be the last MLB tiebreaker games.

33. It was a replay at New York of a tie between the Cubs and Giants in the famous "Merkle's Boner" game. The Cubs won, 4–2.

34. It was an extra game, at home, added to break the tie for first in the division between the Cubs and Brewers. The Cubs lost, 3–1.

35. In 1998, at home against the Giants. The Cubs won, 5–3.

36. Most wins in a season, with 116. It was tied once, by the Mariners in 2001, but never surpassed. They also had the highest winning percentage ever, .763, as they lost 36 games and tied three. They are the only team ever to reach 80 games above .500 at any point in a season.

37. Most wins in the span of five seasons, 530.

38. Brewers. Cubs lost at home, 4–2. They won the next two games, 9–5 and 4–3, respectively.

39. Cleveland, where they lost, 7–6, on August 29, 1997. It was their first game at Cleveland since an 11–2 win over the Spiders, on May 5, 1899. Fun fact: The 1899 Spiders went 20–134, and the Cubs played them 14 times that season. The May 5 game was their only loss.

40. Kansas City Cowboys, nine games in 1886, the Cowboys' only season; and St. Louis Browns, today's Cardinals, in the final game of 1892.

41. Reds, in the "Field of Dreams" Game at Dyersville, in 2022.

42. Six games—two each at Tokyo against the Mets (in 2000) and the Dodgers (2025), and two at London against the Cardinals (in 2023).

43. New York (several parks in Brooklyn, by far the most at Ebbets Field), New Jersey (Roosevelt Stadium in Jersey City) and California (Los Angeles Memorial Coliseum and Dodger Stadium).

44. Carmen Fanzone.

45. Bill Faul.

46. Andre Dawson.

47. Frank Schulte (1912), Rogers Hornsby (1929), Hack Wilson (1930), Gabby Hartnett (1935), Phil Cavarretta (1945), Hank Sauer (1952), Ernie Banks (1958 and 1959), Ryne Sandberg (1984), Andre Dawson (1987), Sammy Sosa (1998), and Kris Bryant (2016).

48. Ferguson Jenkins (1971), Bruce Sutter (1979), Rick Sutcliffe (1984), Greg Maddux (1992), and Jake Arrieta (2015).

49. Billy Williams (1961), Ken Hubbs (1962), Jerome Walton (1989), Kerry Wood (1998), Geovany Soto (2008), and Kris Bryant (2015).

50. Danny Murphy, on June 18, 1960, when he went 0-for-4 while leading off and playing center field at Cincinnati. Murphy played 49 games for the Cubs over parts of three seasons and slashed .171/.221/.301. In 1969–70, he pitched in 68 games for the White Sox, going 4–4 with a 4.66 ERA.

51. Dick Ellsworth, at 18 years, ninety-two days on June 21, 1958, when he started at Cincinnati. In 2 1/3 innings, he gave up four runs—all earned—on four hits and three walks, and did not strike out a batter. In eight seasons as a Cub, Ellsworth went 84–110 with a 3.70 ERA, though he had one spectacular season, 1963, in which he went 22–10 with a 2.11 ERA. The 10.2 bWAR Ellsworth posted in 1963 is tied for the second-best by a Cubs pitcher in the Live Ball Era with Fergie Jenkins (1971).

52. Phil Cavarretta: 277 games from 1934–36. He was 18 years, 59 days old on September 16, 1934, when he made his debut by striking out as a pinch-hitter at Brooklyn.

53. Hoyt Wilhelm, who was 48 years, 68 days old on September 28, 1970, when he pitched against the Mets in the last of three games for the Cubs. In two-thirds of an inning, he gave up three runs, all earned, on two hits including a home run. He walked onc and struck out none. Wilhelm was 49 years, 350 days when he pitched his final big-league game, for the Phillies, on July 10, 1972.

54. Gary Gaetti, 113 games, in 1999. He slashed .204/.260 /.339.

55. Davey Lopes, 99 games in 1985, when he turned 40; Justin Turner, 80 games in 2025, when he turned 40; and Walker Cooper, 54 games in 1955, when he turned 40. Lopes played 59 games in 1986, when he turned 41.

56. Koji Uehara, 49 games in 2017, when he turned 42; Dutch Leonard, 45 games in 1952, when he turned 43, and 1953, when he turned 44; and 41 games in 1951, when he turned 41. Next most is 36 games by Charlie Root in 1940, when he turned 41.

57. Animalistic: 1-G, 2-C, 3-F, 4-A, 5-H, 6-D, 7-B, 8-E.

One-Name Wonders: 1-C, 2-H, 3-A, 4-L, 5-J, 6-E, 7-B, 8-G, 9-K, 10-D, 11-O&M, 12-F, 13-I, 14-N.

Leadership: 1-B, 2-G, 3-A, 4-D, 5-C&F, 6-E.

Other Dandies: 1-C, 2-G, 3-A, 4-D, 5-F, 6-B, 7-E.

58. The Cubs, then known as White Stockings, first played in 23rd Street Park (sometimes called 23rd Street Grounds), located near the corner of what is now 23rd Street and State Street. They played there for just two seasons, 1876–77, posting a 42–18 record there.

59. The Cubs, then still "White Stockings," were playing in Lakefront Park, a curiously designed field that was more a long rectangle than the type of baseball fields we know now. In that park, the left-field fence was 180 feet from home plate and the right-field fence was just 196 feet away. Before 1884, a ball hit over the fence had been a double, not a home run, but for that one season that rule was changed. The result was predictable: the team hit 131 of their 142 homers at home, where their record was 39–17. They were 23–33 on the road and finished fifth, 22 games behind league champion Providence.

60. Ed Williamson, sometimes known as "Ned" Williamson. He hit 25 of his 27 at home. Williamson never hit more than nine home runs in any of his other 12 major-league seasons.

61. A judge ruled that having a business operating on the city-owned land violated the terms of the agreement under which the land had been donated. The team moved to the West Side, in the first of two parks they would inhabit there. West Side Park, located near what is now the intersection of Congress and Throop Streets, was the Cubs' home from 1885–91.

62. South Side Park II, which was built for a team in the Players' League. That league operated for only one season, 1890, after which the Cubs played some of their home schedule there from 1891–93. In 1891, they played only Tuesday, Thursday, and Saturday games there, with the others at West Side Park, then the team played its entire home schedule at South Side Park II in 1892–93.

63. Pat Pieper, who missed 16 games over 59 seasons. He began with a hefty megaphone. An electronic public address system was introduced in 1932. Pieper had begun working for the Cubs as a vendor in 1905, and worked as the PA announcer from 1916 until his death following the 1974 season.

64. Before each game, Pieper would precede the lineup announcement by saying, "Attention! . . . Attention, please! . . . Have your pencil . . . and scorecards ready . . . and I'll give you . . . the correct lineup . . . for today's ballgame."

One of the reasons he said "the correct lineup" is that the Wrigley Field scorecard, up to 1955, had a preprinted lineup. Many times, of course, there were changes to that preprinted lineup and so the "correct" lineup was the one presented on the PA system by Pieper.

A recording of Pieper's famous announcement is played each day at Wrigley Field before current PA announcer Jeremiah Paprocki gives the lineup.

65. Gene Baker who, at 28, was six years older than Banks. Both had been shortstops in the minors. Baker was moved to second base by the Cubs, and made the NL All-Star team in 1955. Injuries reduced his effectiveness and he was traded to the Pirates in 1957. He got a World Series ring with the Pirates in 1960 and the following year became the first Black manager in Organized Baseball when the Pirates named him manager at their Batavia team in the New York-Penn League.

66. Banks moved to left field, which he played for 23 games before moving again, to first base, where he remained through 1971, when he played his final game, with the exception of eight games played at third base in 1966 under manager Leo Durocher, who was trying many different combinations in his first year managing the Cubs.

67. Second baseman Ross Barnes, at Cincinnati, on May 2, 1876, in their fourth NL game, a 15–9 victory. It was Barnes's only home in 88 games during two seasons with the Cubs, then the White Stockings. The team hit eight homers in 1876, including two each by Cap Anson and Paul Hines. Barnes led the NL in 1876 in WAR, runs, hits, doubles, triples walks, batting average, on-base percentage, slugging and on-base plus slugging. Had an MVP award existed then, he surely would have won it.

One of the reasons Barnes hit so well in 1876 was the presence of a rule called the "fair-foul rule," which stated that a ball that was hit fair, then bounced foul, was considered a hit. Barnes got quite adept at this, enough so that the rule was changed the following year – with Barnes' numbers suffering accordingly. He played in just 22 games in 1877, hit poorly, and left the Cubs (then, of course, "White Stockings") after that year, playing again only briefly for Boston in 1881.

68. Shortstop John Peters vs. Boston on July 13, 1876, in their 17th home game. It was Peters's only homer of the season. He hit one more in his three seasons with the Cubs.

69. Max Flack vs. Cincinnati on April 22, 1916, in the Cubs' second game at their new home, then called Weeghman Park.

It wasn't the first home run in the park, though. That honor went to Johnny Beall of the Reds, who homered in the very first Cubs game at what is now Wrigley Field in the first game of 1916, on April 20. A local tailor had offered a free suit to the first player who homered in the Cubs' new park, though there was never a report on whether the tailor gave the suit to Beall.

70. Center fielder Bill Lange, who quit after seven seasons, all with the Cubs, in which he batted .330/.400/.458, for an OPS of .858, with 23.2 bWAR. He also stole 400 bases, 290 of them from 1894–97.

The marriage lasted only a bit more than twice as long as Lange's baseball career. He and his wife Grace, who married in 1900, were divorced in 1915. Lange later married two more times and had a son, and one of his nephews, George "High Pockets" Kelly, played briefly for the Cubs in 1930.

71. Harry Steinfeldt was the Cubs' third baseman for most of the Tinker-Evers-Chance era. He was acquired in a trade from the Reds after the 1905 season, leading the National League with 176 hits and 83 RBIs in the Cubs' 116-win pennant season in 1906. The Cubs won three more pennants with Steinfeldt at third base from 1908–10, but his performance began to decline by 1910, and he was let go. He played briefly again for the Reds in 1911 and sadly, died of a cerebral hemorrhage in 1914, aged just 38.

72. Johnny Kling was the catcher for the Tinker-Evers-Chance years. Kling sat out the 1909 season in a salary dispute. He felt he could make more money running a pool hall in his hometown of Kansas City, and given the baseball economics of the time, he was likely correct. The 1909 season was the only one between 1906 and 1910 in which the Cubs did not win the National League pennant, despite winning 104 games. It's possible Kling's absence cost the team a chance at five straight league pennants.

73. Frank "Wildfire" Schulte, Jimmy Sheckard, and Jimmy Slagle, then Solly Hofman, were the primary outfielders during the Cubs' pennant years from 1906–10.

Schulte was named National League MVP in 1911, but the Cubs finished second, 7 1/2 games behind the pennant-winning Giants.

74. The famed Cubs teammates were all elected to the Hall of Fame by the Old Timers Committee in 1946. Just two of them lived to see the honor, as Chance had died in 1924. Evers died in 1947; Tinker, in 1948.

75. The poem, written by Franklin P. Adams, goes as follows:

These are the saddest of possible words:
"Tinker to Evers to Chance."
Trio of bear cubs, and fleeter than birds,
Tinker and Evers and Chance.
Ruthlessly pricking our gonfalon bubble,
Making a Giant hit into a double –
Words that are heavy with nothing but trouble:
"Tinker to Evers to Chance."

76. A "gonfalon" is another name for a pennant or flag, thus the poem was lamenting the double plays the three Cubs would make against the Giants, hurting New York's pennant chances.

In reality, the 1910 Cubs finished in the middle of the pack in double plays with 110. What Adams might have been reacting to was a Cubs-Giants game two days earlier at the Polo Grounds, in which Tinker, Evers, and Chance turned a key double play in the eighth inning, squelching a Giants rally and helping the Cubs post a 4–2 victory.

77. Between 1902 and 1911, the years that Tinker, Evers, and Chance were Cubs teammates, they turned 71 double plays that went in that order. They also made 50 that went Evers to Tinker to Chance and one each that went Tinker to Chance to Evers and Evers to Chance to Tinker. They made a total of 250 that involved at least one of the three and no one else, of which 37 were against the Giants. Tinker, Evers and Chance played in 728 games together.

78. Ryne Sandberg, third in WAR at 68.1 (acquired from the Phillies in 1982 along with Larry Bowa for Ivan de Jesus).

Sammy Sosa, sixth at 58.8 (acquired from the White Sox in 1992 along with Ken Patterson for George Bell).

Ferguson Jenkins, eighth at 54.8 (acquired from the Phillies in 1966 along with John Herrnstein and Adolfo Phillips for Bob Buhl and Larry Jackson).

Mordecai "Three Finger" Brown, 11th at 48.0 (acquired from the Cardinals in 1903 along with Jack O'Neill for Larry McLean and Jack Taylor).

Grover Cleveland Alexander, 16th at 43.2 (acquired from the Phillies in 1917 along with Bill Killefer for Pickles Dillhoefer, Mike Prendergast, and $55,000).

Hippo Vaughn, 19th at 40.5 (acquired from Kansas City of the American Association in 1913 for Lew Richie).

Anthony Rizzo, 24th at 37.1 (acquired from the Padres in 2012 with minor leaguer Zach Cates for Andrew Cashner and minor leaguer Kyung-Min Na).

79. Billy Williams, third-most games with 2,213 (to the Athletics in 1974 for Darold Knowles, Bob Locker, and Manny Trillo).

Ron Santo, fifth most with 2,126 (to the White Sox in 1973 for Ken Frailing, Steve Stone, Steve Swisher, and a player to be named later, who turned out to be Jim Kremmel).

Sammy Sosa, 10th most with 1,811 (to the Orioles in 2005 with cash for Mike Fontenot, Jerry Hairston, and minor leaguer Dave Crouthers).

Don Kessinger, 12th most with 1,648 (to the Cardinals in 1975 for Mike Garman and a player to be named later, who turned out to be minor leaguer Bobby Hrapmann).

Frank Schulte, 13th with 1,564 (to the Pirates in 1916 with William Fischer for Art Wilson).

Joe Tinker, 14th with 1,539 (to the Reds, in 1912 with Harry Chapman and Grover Lowdermilk for Red Corriden, Bert Humphries, Pete Knisely, Mike Mitchell, and Art Phelan).

Johnny Evers, 15th with 1,409 (to the Braves in 1914 for Bill Sweeney and cash).

Bill Nicholson, 16th with 1,349 (to the Phillies in 1948 for Harry Walker).

Billy Herman, 17th with 1,344 (to the Dodgers in 1941 for Charlie Gilbert, Johnny Hudson, and $65,000).

Anthony Rizzo, 19th with 1,308 (to the Yankees in 2021 with cash for Kevin Alcántara and minor leaguer Alexander Vizcaino).

Glenn Beckert, 22nd with 1,247 (to the Padres in 1973 with Bobby Fenwick for Jerry Morales).

Woody English, 26th with 1,098 (to the Dodgers in 1936 with Roy Henshaw for Lonny Frey).

Billy Jurges, 28th with 1,072 (to the Giants in 1938 with Frank Demaree and Kevin O'Dea for Dick Bartell, Hank Leiber, and Gus Mancuso; Jurges had played 976 games as a Cub at the time. He rejoined the team as a free agent in 1946 and played 96 games that year and the next).

Johnny Kling, 30th with 1,025 (to the Braves in 1911 with Hank Griffin, Al Kaiser, and Orlie Weaver for Bill Collins, Cliff Curtis, Wilbur Good, and Peaches Graham).

Heinie Zimmerman, 31st with 1,022 (to the Giants in 1916 for Larry Doyle, Herb Hunter, and Merwin Jacobson).

80. During years when neither team was in the World Series, the Cubs played the White Sox in what was dubbed the "City Series." The Cubs won six series, the Sox won eighteen and one ended in a tie.

81. This game was played to benefit Frank Selee, who had managed Boston from 1890–1901 and the Cubs since 1902. He had forced to leave the team due to ill health in late July 1905 and never returned. The benefit game raised $3,640.25, equivalent to $134,377.21 today. The Cubs sent $640.25 to Selee and deposited the remaining $3,000 in a trust fund that would pay Selee $125 per month. Selee died in 1909, aged just 49.

82. Team president Albert Spalding wanted to promote baseball around the world, so he had his club embark on a world tour, during which they went 22–28–3 against a team of top players from other National League clubs. They played games in New Zealand, Australia, Sri Lanka, Egypt, Italy, France, England, Scotland and Ireland, plus eight US cities before crossing the Pacific Ocean and nine after crossing the Atlanta. The tour began on October 20 and lasted exactly six months, through April 20. The team began the 1889 NL season four days later, and the tour likely exhausted them, as they finished third, 19 games out of first place.

83. The Cubs trained in Tampa from 1913–16. Then they moved spring camp to California, in Pasadena from 1917–21 and Catalina Island beginning in 1922. They would remain on Catalina until 1951, with the exception of 1943–45 when major-league teams were not permitted to train south of the Mason-Dixon line or west of the Mississippi. For those years, Cubs camp was in French Lick, Indiana.

84. After their 100-win season in 1935, the Cubs thought they could cash in on the team's popularity. Thus they began spring training in California on February 18, then starting March 17 played 19 games in 22 days in 17 cities in six states: El Paso and Houston, Texas; New Orleans; Pensacola, Florida; Selma and Dothan, Alabama; Tallahassee, Lakeland, Tampa, St. Petersburg, Bradenton, Clearwater, Winter Haven, and Sarasota, Florida; Thomasville, Georgia; and Montgomery and Birmingham, Alabama Games scheduled to be played in Gadsden, Alabama, and Nashville, Tennessee, were rained out.

85. Cubs spring camps have been held in Arizona, Arkansas, California, Georgia, Illinois, Indiana, Louisiana, Mississippi, and Missouri.

86. The Cubs were the spring training tenant at Scottsdale Stadium in Scottsdale, Arizona from 1967–78, when they returned to Mesa. Previously, Scottsdale Stadium had been the spring home of the Baltimore Orioles (1956–58) and Boston Red Sox (1959–65). After the Cubs departed, the Oakland A's held spring camp in Scottsdale from 1979–83, and it has been the spring home of the San Francisco Giants since 1984. The park underwent major renovations in 1992 and 2006.

87. During the World War I and II years, the Cubs played exhibition games against a team from Great Lakes Naval Station. They went 1–0 in 1918 and 1–5 in 1942–45.

88. That game took place in 1995 against the Detroit Tigers in the Hall of Fame Game at Cooperstown, New York. Scott Bullett and Howard Johnson both homered twice and the Cubs won 8–6. The Cubs also played in Cooperstown vs. the Red Sox, in 1940, and the Indians, in 1952, 1960, 1971, and 1988. They were scheduled to play in the final Hall of Fame Game in 2008 against the Padres, and did make it to Cooperstown for a parade, but the game was rained out.

89. The Cubs' most recent in-season exhibition game was an 8–0 victory at Tinker Field in Orlando over the Southern League All-Stars, on May 30, 1996. It was the last of 244 in-season exhibition games the Cubs played. During the game. Cubs outfielder Scott Bullett hit a home run that landed in the Citrus Bowl football stadium, which was adjacent to Tinker Field.

ONE AND DONE

90. Joe Tinker, nine. Solly Hofman and Billy Williams did it seven times; Frank Chance and Andy Pafko, six.

91. The Cubs had 56 of their 258 1–0 wins on a solo home run, or 21.7 percent.

92. Ernie Banks and Andy Pafko.

93. Phil Cavarretta, Rick Monday, Ryne Sandberg, and Kyle Schwarber.

94. Juan Pizarro on September 16, 1971 at New York against the Mets. It came with one out in the eighth inning off future Hall of Famer Tom Seaver. Pizarro completed a six-hitter with two walks and eight strikeouts. It was one of three shutouts Pizarro threw for the Cubs in 1971. This one turned out to be the last one of 17 blankings he threw in his 18-year major-league career.

95. Double and sacrifice fly.

96. A double play in the first inning at St. Louis on July 25, 1919. They have won two games by 1–0 on steals of home and two more on groundouts that drove in the run.

97. Thirty-seven of the 258 1–0 Cubs wins have been walk-offs, or 14.3 percent. The most recent such game happened July 3, 2025, a 1–0 win over the Guardians in 10 innings.

98. Thirteen—nine in the ninth inning and one each in the 10th, 11th, and 12th. The most recent was by Chris Denorfia against the Royals in the 11th inning on September 28, 2015. Frank Schulte homered for a 1–0 win in the 12th at Pittsburgh on July 1, 1912.

WALK THE WALK

99. As of the end of 2025, the Cubs have 950 walk-off wins at home and 47 on the road batting second, which was permitted in the early days of baseball. The last of the 47 was in 1896.

100. A total of 794 of the 950 walk-off Cubs wins at home have happened at Wrigley Field. The most recent, as of the end of 2025, happened September 1, 2025, a 7–6, 10-inning win over the Braves.

101. The Phillies, who the Cubs have walked off 119 times. They have 115 vs. the Dodgers, 112 each vs. the Braves and Giants, 109 vs. the Reds, 103 vs. the Cardinals, and 100 vs. the Pirates. Their most against any of the expansion teams is 36 vs. the Mets, followed by 27 vs. the Astros and 26 vs. the

Padres. They also have 26 vs. American League teams. The most against any AL team is six, over both the White Sox and Indians/Guardians.

102. Ron Santo had the last at-bat in a walk-off win 17 times; Mark Grace, 15; Ernie Banks and Sammy Sosa, 13; Gabby Hartnett, Riggs Stephenson, and Billy Williams, 11.

103. Extra innings, 540 to 457.

104. The longest was a 21-inning win over the Phillies on July 17, 1918. Max Flack's nobody-out, bases-loaded single gave the Cubs a 2–1 win. They won three walk-offs in the 19th inning: 3–2 vs. the Pirates in 1902, 4–3 vs. the Dodgers in 1915, and 3–2 vs. the Braves in 1932.

105. The Cubs have 195 walk-off home runs.

106. The Cubs have 34 wins on walk-off walks.

107. The Cubs have six wins on walk-off hit by pitches, the most recent coming September 16, 2020, at Wrigley Field, when Cameron Maybin was plunked with the bases loaded in the 10th inning.

108. The Cubs' only win on a walk-off balk came in the 12th inning against the Giants on July 11, 1896.

BATTERS

QUESTIONS

CAREER

1. Who played the most regular-season games as a Cub?
   Answer on page 49.

2. Name the four others who played at least 2,000.
   Answer on page 49.

3. Ian Happ has played 1,139 games as a Cub (through the end of the 2025 season), the third most by any Cub who never played for another team. Name the two who played more.
   Answer on page 49.

4. Who made the most hits as a Cub?
   Answer on page 49.

5. Name the two others who made at least 2,500.
   Answer on page 50.

6. Who compiled the highest batting average as a Cub?
   Answer on page 50.

7. Name the 10 others who averaged at least .300.
Answer on page 50.

8. Who hit the most home runs as a Cub?
Answer on page 50.

9. Name the three others who hit at least 250.
Answer on page 50.

10. Who hit the most home runs as a Cub before the Modern Era began in 1901?
Answer on page 50.

11. Who hit the most home runs before World War II?
Answer on page 50.

12. Who stole the most bases as a Cub?
Answer on page 50.

13. Who stole the most among players whose careers began in the Modern Era?
Answer on page 51.

SEASON

14. Which Cubs played the most games in one season?
Answer on page 51.

15. Who was the last Cub to play 162 games in one season?
Answer on page 51.

16. Which Cub had the most hits in one season?
Answer on page 51.

17. Which player collected the most hits in a season after 1936?
Answer on page 51.

18. Name the five Cubs who led the National League in hits in a season.
Answer on page 52.

19. Which Cub had the longest hitting streak?
Answer on page 52.

20. Who had the highest batting average in a season of the Modern Era?
Answer on page 52.

21. Who had the highest since 1930?
Answer on page 52.

22. Who had the highest after 1945?
Answer on page 52.

23. Which Cub set a National League record for home runs in a season that was not broken for 68 years?
Answer on page 52.

24. Name the eight Cubs who led the league in home runs in at least one season.
Answer on page 53.

25. Which Cub hit a walk-off grand slam in the 14th inning on the same day in 1980 that he made two hits for Cleveland in a game at Baltimore?
Answer on page 53.

26. Name the four Cubs who have hit walk-off grand slams since then, raising the total to 13.
Answer on page 54.

27. Which Cub stole the most bases in a season?
Answer on page 55.

28. Which stole the most bases in a season of the Modern Era?
Answer on page 55.

29. Which stole the most in a season after 1905?
Answer on page 55.

30. Which Cub set a National League record, later broken, for most consecutive games played?
Answer on page 55.

31. Which Cub set a National League record, later broken, for most consecutive errorless games by a second baseman?
Answer on page 55.

GAME

32. Name the five Cubs who made six hits in a game.
Answer on page 56.

33. Which one of the five did it in a regulation-length game?
Answer on page 56.

34. Name the only two Cubs who hit four doubles in a game.
Answer on page 56.

35. No Cub has hit four home runs in a game. Twenty-seven different Cubs have hit three homers a total of 42 times. Name the seven who did it more than once.
Answer on page 56.

36. Name the four Cubs who walked five times in a game. Which one of the five did it in a regulation-length game? Which one was walked intentionally all five times?
Answer on page 57.

37. Which Cub stole five bases in a game?
Answer on page 57.

38. Who was the last Cub to wear No. 14 before Ernie Banks?
Answer on page 58.

39. Who was the last Cub to wear No. 23 before Ryne Sandberg?
Answer on page 58.

40. Which Cub third baseman's nickname rhymed with his actual given name?
Answer on page 59.

41. A Cubs player led the National League in an offensive category in 1930. After that no Cubs player would have as many of that category until 1978. Name the player and the category he led.
Answer on page 59.

42. Which Cub was traded between games of a doubleheader?
Answer on page 59.

43. Frank Chance set the Cubs' Modern Era record of 67 stolen bases way back in 1903. Who stole the most for the Cubs since then?
Answer on page 60.

BATTERS

ANSWERS

CAREER

1. Ernie Banks played the most games as a Cub, with 2,528.

2. The other four Cubs who played in at least 2,000 games for the team are Cap Anson (2,277), Billy Williams (2,213), Ryne Sandberg (2,151), and Ron Santo (2,126). Of the five (including Banks), Banks is the only one to have played all his career games with the Cubs.

3. Ernie Banks with 2,528 over 19 seasons; and Stan Hack with 1,938 games over 16 seasons. Hack is probably the best third baseman not in the Hall of Fame, with 55.2 bWAR and playing in four World Series in which he batted .348/.408/.449 in 18 games. The Cubs didn't win any of those Fall Classics, but that certainly wasn't Hack's fault!

4. Cap Anson had 3,012 hits in 22 seasons with the Cubs, and overall is credited with 3,435 major-league hits, which as of the end of the 2025 season ranked seventh all-time.

5. Besides Anson, the two Cubs who had 2,500 or more hits with the team are Ernie Banks (2,583) and Billy Williams (2,510).

6. Bill Madlock and Riggs Stephenson both had career numbers of .336 as Cubs (minimum 1,500 plate appearances).

7. The other Cubs with at least a .300 lifetime BA with the team are Ray Grimes (.331), Kiki Cuyler (.325), Hack Wilson (.322), Frank Demaree and Billy Herman (.309), Mark Grace (.308), Charlie Hollocher and Heinie Zimmerman (304), Stan Hack (.301), and Bill Buckner (.300).

8. Sammy Sosa hit 545 home runs as a Cub, eclipsing Ernie Banks's previous team record of 512.

9. The other three Cubs who hit at least 250 home runs in blue pinstripes are Billy Williams (392), Ron Santo (337), and Ryne Sandberg (282). As of the end of the 2025 season, the active leader in home runs as a Cub is Ian Happ, who has 173—good for 15th place on the franchise list. With one more, Happ will tie Andre Dawson for 14th place. Happ has averaged 22 home runs a year from, 2021–25. If he hits that many in 2026, he'll move up to 11th place.

10. The most home runs by a Cub pre–Modern Era (before 1901) was 99 by Jimmy Ryan, who played for the Cubs franchise from 1885 to 1900. He led the National League with 16 in 1888 and hit a career-high 17 the following year.

11. Gabby Hartnett, who was the catcher for four Cubs World Series teams and the manager of the 1938 NL pennant winners, hit 231 home runs for the Cubs before World War II. Second was Hack Wilson, who hit 190.

12. Frank Chance, who played for and managed four Cubs pennant-winning teams from 1906–10 and managed them to two World Series titles, stole 402 bases for the club, the franchise record.

13. The most stolen bases for any Cub whose career began in the Modern Era (post-1900; Chance's began in 1898) is 344, by Ryne Sandberg. Sandberg is also the only Cub in the Modern Era to have five consecutive seasons of 30 or more steals (1982–86).

SEASON

14. The Cubs played two tie games in 1965. Back then, games that were tied and called for darkness at Wrigley Field were deemed to be completed, but also had to be made up in their entirety, though the stats from the tied games counted. That year, Ron Santo and Billy Williams played in all 162 games played to a decision, including the makeups for the two ties, as well as the tie games, so they co-hold the franchise record of 164 games played in a season.

15. Only one player in MLB history has played in more than 164 games in a season: Maury Wills, who played in all 162 scheduled games for the Dodgers in 1962, as well as all three of a pennant playoff against the Giants.

In the divisional play era, just five Cubs have played in at least 162 games in a season. The most is 163, by Billy Williams in 1969 (including one tie game). The last Cub to play 162 games in a season was Starlin Castro, who did so in 2012.

16. Rogers Hornsby holds the Cubs' franchise record for hits in a season with 229 in 1929. The Cubs won the NL pennant that year, and Hornsby's 10.6 bWAR is the best season in that category for any Cubs position player.

17. In the high-offense 1930s, six other Cubs had 200 or more hits in a season, the last of those Billy Herman with 211 in 1936.

Since 1936, the most hits by a Cub in a season is 207 by Starlin Castro in 2011.

18. The five Cubs who led the National League in hits in the Modern Era are Harry Steinfeldt, 1906 (176); Heinie Zimmerman, 1912 (207); Charlie Hollocher, 1918 (161); Billy Herman, 1935 (227); Stan Hack, 1940 (191, tied), and 1941 (186); Phil Cavarretta, 1944 (197, tied); Billy Williams, 1970 (205, tied); Derrek Lee, 2005 (199); Juan Pierre, 2006 (204); and Starlin Castro, 2011 (207).

19. Bill Dahlen, a Cub from 1891–98, hit in 42 consecutive games for the team in 1894. That's also the fourth-longest batting streak by anyone in MLB history. The Modern Era Cubs record for a batting streak is 30 games, set by Jerome Walton in his Rookie of the Year season in 1989.

20. Rogers Hornsby hit .380 in 1929, the all-time record for a Cub in a single season.

21. Since 1930, the best season BA for a Cub is .355, by Phil Cavarretta in 1945, a Cubs pennant-winning season and Cavarretta's sole MVP season.

22. Since 1945, Bill Madlock's .354 season in 1975 is the Cubs' best for a single season, and he followed it up with a league-leading .336 season in 1976. Just one Cub has hit .330 or better since then: Derrek Lee, who batted .335 in 2005.

23. In 1930, a hitters' year in baseball (the entire National League hit .303 that year!), Hack Wilson hit 56 home runs, becoming the first National League player to hit 50 or more. In fact, no other NL player would hit 50 or more until Johnny Mize hit 51 for the Giants in 1947. Wilson's NL record stood for 68 years until Sammy Sosa (66) and Mark McGwire (70) broke it in 1998.

24. The following eight Cubs led the National League in home runs at least once: Frank Schulte (10 in 1910—tied with Fred Beck—and 21 in 1911); Heinie Zimmerman (14 in 1912); Cy Williams (12 in 1916, tied with Dave Robertson); Hack Wilson (four times, 21 in 1926, 30 in 1927, 31 in 1928—tied with Jim Bottomley—and 56 in 1930); Bill Nicholson (twice, 29 in 1943 and 33 in 1944); Hank Sauer (37 in 1952, tied with Ralph Kiner); Ernie Banks (twice, 47 in 1958 and 41 in 1960); Dave Kingman (48 in 1979); Andre Dawson (49 in 1987); Ryne Sandberg (40 in 1990); and Sammy Sosa (twice, 50 in 2000, 49 in 2002).

25. This happened because of the suspended-game rule at Wrigley Field. A game at Wrigley Field between the Cubs and Expos on May 28, 1980, was suspended after 10 innings with the score tied 3–3, to be completed August 8.

On May 28, Cliff Johnson was playing for Cleveland against Baltimore, and was their DH in a 10–6 victory, collecting two hits and scoring a pair of runs.

The Cubs acquired Johnson from Cleveland on June 23 for a player to be named later; a week later Karl Pagel was sent to Cleveland to complete the deal.

When the game resumed, Johnson was on the Cubs' active roster and thus eligible to play in the completion of the suspended game. In the bottom of the 11th, manager Joe Amalfitano—the Cubs' second manager of the game, as Preston Gomez had been fired in the interim—sent Johnson up to pinch-hit for Mike Vail. He struck out, but remained in the game at first base.

Both teams scored in the 12th, but not in the 13th or 14th. Montreal failed to score in the top of the 15th, and in the bottom of the inning the Cubs loaded the bases with a one-out walk (drawn by pitcher Dennis Lamp!), a force play, a single and intentional walk.

That brought up Johnson, who ran the count to 3-1. A walk would have won the game for the Cubs, so Expos pitcher Dale Murray threw a strike and Johnson hit a walk-off grand slam, the Cubs winning the game 8–4. Since statistics of suspended games are considered to have officially happened on the date the game started, Johnson played for two teams that won their games on May 28, 1980, even though one of them finished over two months later.

26. The four Cubs who have hit walk-off grand slams since 1980 are:

August 30, 1993 (11th inning): Rick Wilkins against the Phillies. This was one of 30 homers Wilkins hit in what turned out to be a fluke year and it came after the Cubs overcame a 6–3 deficit. The first two men had been retired in the 11th before Mark Grace walked, Derrick May singled and Sammy Sosa walked to load the bases.

July 27, 2009 (13th inning): Alfonso Soriano against the Astros. Soriano's slam ended a game that had dragged on in a 1–1 tie for nearly four hours (the only Cubs run up to that point was a Derrek Lee homer). The win put the Cubs in first place in the NL Central.

June 6, 2018: Jason Heyward against the Phillies. The game was tied 3–3 going into the ninth inning when Philadelphia's Dylan Cozens hit a two-run homer off Brandon Morrow. That would turn out to be Cozens's only MLB home run. In the bottom of the ninth, the Cubs loaded the bases with one out, but Ben Zobrist hit into a force play at the plate. Heyward ran the count to 2-2 before smacking his walk-off slam.

August 12, 2018: David Bote, against the Nationals. This was known as an "ultimate" grand slam, defined as a walk-off grand slam with your team down by three runs with two out in the bottom of the ninth. The Cubs had managed just four hits before the ninth, but loaded the bases on a single and two batters being hit by a pitch before Bote's slam.

27. Frank Chance, who holds the franchise record for stolen bases in a career, also holds the single-season Cubs stolen-base record, with 67 in 1903.

28. No Cubs player has stolen 60 bases in a season since then; the most is 59 by Billy Maloney in 1905.

29. Since 1905, the most by any Cub in a season is 58 by Juan Pierre in 2006.

30. Billy Williams played in 1,117 consecutive games from September 22, 1963, through September 2, 1970. The streak might have lasted longer, but Williams had tired of it and asked manager Leo Durocher for a day off.

The streak might also have lasted longer if Cubs head coach Bob Kennedy hadn't given Williams a day off against future Hall of Famer Warren Spahn on September 21, 1963. Williams had played in all 155 games in 1963 before that day off, as well as the last 50 games of the 1962 season. So if not for that rest day, Williams's streak could have been as long as 1,323 games.

Billy's league record streak was broken by Steve Garvey in the 1980s. Garvey now holds the National League record with 1,207 consecutive games played. His streak was ended by an injury in 1983.

31. Cubs rookie second baseman Ken Hubbs played in 78 consecutive errorless games in 1962, breaking a major-league record previously held by Bobby Doerr of the Red Sox (73 games in 1948). Hubbs's promising career ended tragically in a plane crash in 1964 when he was just 22. The consecutive game streak was broken by Placido Polanco, who did not commit an error in 186 straight games over three seasons from 2006–08.

GAME

32. Frank Demaree (July 5, 1937, first game); Don Kessinger (June 17, 1971); Bill Madlock (July 26, 1975); José Cardenal (May 2, 1976, first game); and Sammy Sosa (July 2, 1993) are the five Cubs who have had six hits in a game.

33. Sammy Sosa is the only Cub to have six hits in a nine-inning game. He did it July 2, 1993, against the Rockies at Mile High Stadium in Denver. He doubled in the first inning, then hit five singles, in the third, fifth, sixth, seventh and ninth, driving in two runs and scoring twice. The Cubs won the game, 11–8.

34. Billy Williams hit four doubles against the Phillies on April 9, 1969, at Wrigley Field. One of the doubles came as part of a seven-run seventh that helped put the game away. The Cubs won, 11–2, with Williams driving in two of the runs.

Matt Murton doubled four times against the Diamondbacks in the second game of a doubleheader August 3, 2006. Two of those were two-run doubles and Murton had five RBIs in a 7–3 Cubs win. Incidentally, that doubleheader occupies an interesting place in Cubs history: It is the most recent single-admission doubleheader at Wrigley Field.

35. The seven Cubs who have homered three times in a game at least twice are:

Hank Sauer (two times): August 28, 1950 (first game) vs. Phillies; June 11, 1952, vs. Phillies.

Ernie Banks (four times): August 4, 1955 vs. Pirates; September 14, 1957 (second game) vs. Pirates; May 29, 1962 vs. Braves; June 9, 1963 vs. Dodgers.

Dave Kingman (three times): May 14, 1978 vs. Dodgers; May 17, 1979 vs. Phillies; July 28, 1979 vs. Mets.

Sammy Sosa (six times): June 5, 1996 vs. Phillies; June 15,

1998 vs. Brewers; August 9, 2001 vs. Rockies; August 22, 2001 vs. Brewers; September 23, 2001 vs. Astros; August, 10, 2002 vs. Rockies.

Aramis Ramirez (two times): July 30, 2004 vs. Phillies; September 16, 2004 vs. Reds.

Alfonso Soriano (two times): June 8, 2007 vs. Braves; September 6, 2008 vs. Reds.

Kris Bryant (two times): June 27, 2016 vs. Reds; May 17, 2009 vs. Nationals.

36. The four Cubs who drew five walks in a game are:

Rogers Hornsby, August 5, 1929, in a 9–8 win over the Dodgers.

Elrod Hendricks, September 16, 1972, in an 18–5 win over the Mets.

Andre Dawson, May 22, 1990, in a 2–1 win over the Reds.

Eric Young Sr., June 30, 2000, in a 7–4 win over the Brewers.

The only one of those four who did it in a regulation-length game was Hendricks. The Mets starter was future Hall of Famer Tom Seaver, who walked eight—the only time Seaver ever walked eight in a game.

The only one of those four whose walks were all intentional was Dawson. He had been on a tremendous hot streak, batting .396/.393/.943 with eight home runs in his previous 13 games and the Reds simply did not want to allow him to beat them. The game had gone scoreless for 12 innings and each team scored once in the 13th. The Reds intentionally walked Dawson in the first (!), eighth, 12th, 14th, and 16th innings. The last of those happened with first base occupied (Mark Grace) and Ryne Sandberg on third, loading the bases for Dave Clark, who hit a game-winning single.

37. You might think this answer would be a player from the Deadball Era, but it took until 2000 for a Cub to steal five bases in a game. That's Eric Young Sr., who did it May 14, 2000, in a game against the Expos at Montreal. The game had six lead changes, and the Cubs led 15–13 going to the bottom of the ninth, but Rick Aguilera gave up three runs and the Cubs lost, 16–15.

Young went on to have a 54-steal season for the Cubs in 2000, at the time just the second 50-steal season for the Cubs since 1905 (Ryne Sandberg also had 54 in 1985).

38. The last Cub to wear No. 14 before Ernie Banks was Paul Schramka, an outfielder who played in two games for the Cubs in April 1953, one as a pinch-runner, the other as a defensive replacement. Banks was issued the number when he joined the Cubs in September 1953.

Schramka played one more year in the Cubs minor leagues, then returned to his hometown of Milwaukee where he began working for his family's funeral home, a business which continues in Wisconsin to this day.

When Banks was elected to the Hall of Fame in 1982, Schramka sent him a telegram of congratulations and said, "I left all the hits in the jersey for you."

39. Jim Tracy, an outfielder who played in 87 games for the Cubs in 1980 and 1981, batting .249/.336/.368 with three home runs, was the last player to wear No. 23 for the Cubs before Ryne Sandberg.

When Sandberg reported to the Cubs in 1982 after he was acquired from the Phillies, he was asked what number he wanted. He told clubhouse manager Yosh Kawano, who was in charge of issuing numbers, that he would like No. 14, as he had worn that as a high school quarterback in Spokane, Washington. Yosh gently explained to Ryno who Ernie Banks was, told him that No. 14 was going to be retired later that year, and said that

No. 23 was a "fine infielder's number." Now, a No. 23 flag for Sandberg's retired number flies above Wrigley Field along with Banks' No. 14 flag.

Tracy later became a major-league manager, spending 11 seasons managing the Dodgers, Pirates, and Rockies.

Besides Tracy, some of the other men who wore No. 23 before Sandberg include Pete LaCock, Carmen Fanzone, and Don Young.

40. Ransom Joseph Jackson, known for much of his playing career as "Randy," was also nicknamed "Handsome Ransom," obviously for the rhyme.

Jackson played third base for the Cubs from 1950–55, making two National League All-Star teams (1954 and 1955) and overall batting .265/.327/.430 with 88 home runs in 739 games. After the 1955 season he was traded along with Don Elston to the Dodgers for Don Hoak, Russ Meyer, and Walt Moryn. This was one of the rare 1950s trades that worked out all right for the Cubs, as Moryn spent several years in Chicago as a useful left fielder, and the Cubs eventually got Elston back and he had several good years for them in the bullpen.

41. Kiki Cuyler stole 43 bases for the Cubs in 1930. No Cubs player would steal that many until Ivan de Jesus had 44 in 1980.

Cuyler is largely forgotten today, but he was one of the great Cubs hitters of his time, leading the National League in stolen bases three years in a row from 1929–31 and overall batting .325/.391/.485 with 161 steals in eight Cubs seasons, during which they won three NL pennants. He was elected to the Hall of Fame in 1968.

42. Max Flack, an outfielder, had come to the Cubs in 1916 after two years with the Federal League team in Chicago, He had several good years with the Cubs and was a key contributor to their 1918 NL pennant.

Flack got off to a slow start in 1922 and so it was that on May 30 of that year that the Cubs arranged to trade him to the Cardinals for Cliff Heathcote. The Cardinals were playing the Cubs that day at Wrigley Field in a doubleheader and the transaction was completed between games. Both players played for their new teams in the nightcap, Flack going 1-for-4 and Heathcote 2-for-4 as the Cubs won, 3–1.

The Cubs got the better of this deal. Flack was 32 at the time of the trade and was only a part-time player for some mediocre Cardinals teams, retiring before their pennant year in 1926. Heathcote, meanwhile, played nine years for the Cubs and batted .280/.345/.390 with 121 stolen bases and played in two games of the 1929 World Series.

43. The Cubs, over time, have not had many good basestealers. Billy Maloney stole 59 bases in 1905, then it took 80 years until another Cub stole 50 (Ryne Sandberg, 54 in 1985). Eric Young Sr. also had a 54-steal season, in 2000, and Juan Pierre stole 58 in 2006, the most since Maloney. Those three are all the Cubs 50-steal seasons since 1905. Perhaps Pete Crow-Armstrong will join that list someday.

PITCHERS

QUESTIONS

CAREER

1. Who pitched in the most regular-season games as a Cub?
   Answer on page 67.

2. Name the six others who pitched in at least 400.
   Answer on page 67.

3. Who started the most games as a Cub?
   Answer on page 67.

4. Name the three others who started at least 300.
   Answer on page 67.

5. Who relieved in the most games as a Cub?
   Answer on page 68.

6. Name the three others who relieved in at least 400.
   Answer on page 68.

7. Who pitched the most complete games as a Cub?
Answer on page 68.

8. Name the four others who completed at least 150.
Answer on page 68.

9. Who pitched the most shutouts as a Cub?
Answer on page 68.

10. Name the two others who had at least 30 shutouts.
Answer on page 68.

11. Who earned the most saves as a Cub?
Answer on page 68.

12. Name the three others who earned at least 100 saves.
Answer on page 69.

13. Who recorded the most victories as a Cub?
Answer on page 69.

14. Name the four others who won at least 150 games.
Answer on page 69.

15. Who struck out the most batters as a Cub?
Answer on page 69.

16. Name the six others who struck out at least 1,250 batters.
Answer on page 69.

SEASON

17. Name the three pitchers who share the team record for most appearances in a season.
Answer on page 70.

18. Who started the most games in a season during the Modern Era?
Answer on page 70.

19. Name the three others who started at least 40.
Answer on page 70.

20. Who completed the most games in a season during the Modern Era?
Answer on page 70.

21. Who completed the most in a season during the Live Ball Era?
Answer on page 70.

22. Who completed the most in a season after 1945?
Answer on page 70.

23. Who pitched the most shutouts in a season during the Modern Era?
Answer on page 71.

24. Who pitched the most in a season during the Live Ball Era?
Answer on page 71.

25. Who pitched the most in a season after 1945?
Answer on page 71.

26. Who saved the most games in a season?
Answer on page 71.

27. Name the only other pitcher who saved at least 50.
Answer on page 71.

28. Who won the most games in a season during the Modern Era?
Answer on page 72.

29. Who won the most in a season during the Live Ball Era?
Answer on page 72.

30. Who won the most in a season after 1945?
Answer on page 72.

31. Who struck out the most batters in a season?
Answer on page 73.

32. Name the four others with at least 225 after 1901.
Answer on page 73.

GAME

33. No Cub has pitched a perfect game. Who came closest?
Answer on page 73.

34. Name the four others who pitched seven perfect innings.
Answer on page 73.

35. Kerry Wood famously struck out 20 batters against the Astros on May 6, 1998. Who held the previous team record of 17 strikeouts?
Answer on page 74.

36. Name the two Cubs who struck out 16 in a game.
Answer on page 74.

37. Name the five who struck out 15.
Answer on page 74.

38. Name the Cub who pitched a no-hitter in his first game with the team.
Answer on page 74.

39. Name the two Cubs who pitched two no-hitters.
Answer on page 75.

40. Name the last Cub to pitch a no-hitter at Wrigley Field.
Answer on page 75.

41. Name the Cub who pitched a no-hitter neither at Wrigley Field nor the opposing team's home park.
Answer on page 75.

42. Which Cub made the longest start by innings?
Answer on page 76.

43. Which Cub holds the record for longest relief appearance by innings?
Answer on page 76.

PITCHERS

ANSWERS

CAREER

1. Charlie Root is the all-time leader in games pitched for the Cubs, with 605. He was best-known as a starter for three Cubs pennant winners (1929, 1932, 1935), but also threw a lot of games in relief. Just 339 (56 percent) of his 605 games were starts.

2. Besides Root, six other Cubs have appeared in 400 or more games for the team. Four of them are best known as relievers: Carlos Marmol (483), Lee Smith (458), Don Elston (449), and Pedro Strop (401). Two pitchers who were primarily starters complete this group: Guy Bush (428, of which 252 were starts) and Fergie Jenkins (401).

3. Fergie Jenkins's 347 starts over 10 Cubs seasons is the franchise record for games started. He also made 54 relief appearances for the team.

4. Three others besides Fergie Jenkins started more than 300 games for the team: Rick Reuschel (343), Charlie Root (339), and nineteenth-century star Bill Hutchison (also 339).

5. Carlos Marmol holds the Cubs' franchise record for relief appearances with 470. He also made 13 starts for the team, all in 2006.

6. The three pitchers besides Marmol who made 400 or more relief appearances for the Cubs are Lee Smith (452), Don Elston (434), and Pedro Strop (413). Of those, only Strop did not make a single start during his Cubs career. Smith started six times and Elston 15.

7. Mordecai "Three Finger" Brown has the most since 1901, with 206. This is a record that will likely stand forever. For a comparison, there have been 207 complete games in all of MLB since 2020!

8. The five pitchers besides Brown that have had at least 150 complete games in the Modern Era are Charlie Root and Hippo Vaughn (both with 177), Grover Alexander (158), Fergie Jenkins (154) and Bill Lee (153).

Fun fact: Since 1945, the leaders are Jenkins (154), Bob Rush (112), and then Dick Ellsworth, with just 71!

9. Mordecai Brown, a stalwart of the Cubs in the first decade of the twentieth century, threw 48 shutouts for the team—of course, the time was known as the Deadball Era, when run scoring was difficult. Brown had seven shutouts for other teams. His total of 55 ranks tied for 14th all-time, with Steve Carlton.

10. Hippo Vaughn had 35 shutouts for the Cubs in the 1910s, and Ed Reulbach, another pitcher for the early twentieth-century Cubs, had 31. In recent times the most is 29, by Fergie Jenkins.

11. Lee Smith, who collected 180 saves as a Cub from 1980–87. He would finish his career with 478 total saves, and was inducted into the Hall of Fame in 2019.

12. The other three to have at least 100 saves in a Cubs uniform are Bruce Sutter (133), Carlos Marmol (117), and Randy Myers (112).

13. Charlie Root holds the Cubs' franchise record with 201 wins. Oddly, in an era when pitchers made 40-plus starts in a season many times, and 20-win seasons were routine, Root won 20 games only once, in 1927, when he was 26–15 and led the National League with 48 starts and 309 innings.

14. The four Cubs pitchers in the Modern Era who won 150 or more games for the team in addition to Root are: Mordecai Brown (188), Fergie Jenkins (167), Guy Bush (152), and Hippo Vaughn (151).

Of the five, only Root recorded all his wins with the Cubs. He did also pitch one season for the St. Louis Browns (1923, 27 games), but did not record a win for them, going 0–4.

15. The Cubs' franchise record for strikeouts is 2,038, held by Hall of Famer Fergie Jenkins. Jenkins struck out 3,192 batters in his 19-year career, and recorded his 3,000th May 25, 1982, when he struck out Garry Templeton of the Padres. One other pitcher recorded his 3,000th strikeout as a Cub. Greg Maddux did it against the Giants July 26, 2005, striking out Omar Vizquel.

16. Besides Fergie Jenkins, the six other Cubs who struck out at least 1,250 batters with the team are Carlos Zambrano (1,542), Kerry Wood (1,470), Charlie Root (1,432), Rick Reuschel (1,367), Greg Maddux (1,305), and Kyle Hendricks (1,259). All seven also pitched for other teams. The most strikeouts by a Cub who never pitched for another team is 757 by Mark Prior.

SEASON

17. The Cubs' franchise record for games pitched in a season is 84. It was set by Ted Abernathy in 1965, when Abernathy also became the first MLB pitcher to record 30 or more saves in a season (31). The record was tied by Dick Tidrow in 1980 and Bob Howry in 2006.

18. The most games started by any Cubs pitcher in the Modern Era is 42, by Fergie Jenkins in 1969, a year most Cubs fans would agree that manager Leo Durocher probably should have used him a bit less. Jenkins also started 40 games in 1968. Only one MLB pitcher has started more than 42 games in a season since 1978—knuckleballer Phil Niekro, who started 44 in 1979.

19. Besides Jenkins, the three other Cubs who started at least 40 games in a season in the Modern Era are Larry Cheney (40 in 1914), Grover Alexander (40 in 1920), and Bill Hands (41 in 1969). Between Hands and Jenkins, they started more than half (83) of the Cubs' 1969 schedule.

20. The most complete games by any Cub in the Modern Era is 34, by Jack Taylor in 1902. Taylor is best known for completing every one of his starts three times as a Cub: 1899 (39 starts, pre-Modern Era), 1902 (34 starts) and 1903 (33 starts).

21. In the Live Ball Era (1920 to date), the most complete games in a season by any Cubs pitcher is 33, by Grover Cleveland Alexander in . . . 1920. He made 40 starts that year. Unfortunately, it didn't help the Cubs, as they finished fifth in the NL with a 75–79 record.

22. Since 1945, just one Cubs pitcher has completed 30 starts in a season—Fergie Jenkins, who started 39 games in 1971 and completed 30 of them. He threw 325 innings that year and is the last Cubs pitcher to throw 300 or more innings in a season. He won the NL Cy Young Award that year, the first Cubs pitcher to do so, and his 10.1 bWAR season in 1971 ranks as the second-best WAR season by a Cubs pitcher (Grover Cleveland Alexander, 12.0 in 1920, is the best).

23. Four pitchers share the honor of the most shutouts in a season for the Cubs, nine, accomplished five times. They are: Mordecai Brown (1906, 1908), Orval Overall (1909), Grover Cleveland Alexander (1920), and Bill Lee (1938).

24. Bill Lee retains this honor for the Live Ball Era, throwing nine shutouts in 1938. He led the NL in wins (22), ERA (2.66), winning percentage (.710), and bWAR (8.0) that year. No other MLB pitcher had more than five shutouts in 1938.

25. Since 1945, the most shutouts thrown in a season is seven, by Fergie Jenkins in 1969. Ken Holtzman is the only other Cub with at least six since 1945. He accomplished that in 1969. Holtzman's six shutouts that year included his no-hitter against the Braves on August 19, 1969.

26. The most saves in a season by any Cubs pitcher is 53 by Randy Myers in 1993. He had six blown saves that year. Myers had blown three saves in a row in mid-August, and the Cubs had scheduled August 15 as "Randy Myers Poster Day," with that item given away to fans. Myers entered the game in the 11th inning and served up back-to-back homers to Barry Bonds and Matt Williams, after which fans littered the field with the posters. The Cubs lost the game 9–7.

27. Besides Randy Myers, the only other Cub with a 50-save season is "The Shooter," Rod Beck, who saved 51 games in 1998. Beck wound up injured at the end of the season and missed most of 1999, and was never quite as effective after that. The Cubs re-signed him as a free agent in 2003 and assigned him to Triple-A Iowa, where he lived in his RV on the grounds of the I-Cubs stadium. The Cubs could have used him in '03, but they released him in June and he went on to post 20 saves for the Padres.

A 50-save season has become rare in recent years. In the 27 seasons since Beck (and Trevor Hoffman) did it in 1998, there have been just twelve individual seasons of 50 or more saves, with none since 2018.

28. Mordecai Brown holds the Modern Era record for wins in a season for the Cubs with 29 in 1908, the year they won their second straight World Series championship. The 29th and final win was perhaps one of the biggest wins in franchise history, as he out-pitched fellow future Hall of Famer Christy Mathewson in the makeup of the famous "Merkle Game." That happened October 8, 1908, in New York, and the Cubs won, 4–2, to take the NL pennant.

29. In the Live Ball Era (1920 to date), Grover Alexander's 27 wins in 1920 is the most for any Cubs hurler. He went 27–14 and led the NL in many key stat categories, but apart from Alexander and Hippo Vaughn (19–16, 2.54 ERA), the rest of the Cubs pitching staff that year was pretty mediocre and they finished fifth at 75–79.

30. Since 1945, two Cubs pitchers are tied for the honor of most wins in a season. Larry Jackson won 24 in 1964 and Fergie Jenkins matched that figure in 1971. Jenkins won the NL Cy Young Award. In 1964, there was only one Cy Young for both leagues and Dean Chance of the Angels won it. Jackson finished second, and it seems likely that had there been separate league awards then, Jackson would have won the NL Cy Young.

Since Jenkins's 24-win season in 1971, the most wins by a

Cubs pitcher in a season is 22, by Jake Arrieta in 2015. Arrieta, like Jenkins, won the NL Cy Young Award.

31. The most strikeouts in a season by any Cubs pitcher is 314, by Bill Hutchison in 1892. That mark was set the year before the pitching distance was set at its current 60 feet, six inches.

Since then, the most by any Cub is 274, by Fergie Jenkins in 1970.

32. Since 1902 (and that year is chosen since the little-known Tom Hughes had 225 in 1901), the four pitchers who have had at least 225 strikeouts in a season for the Cubs besides Fergie Jenkins are: Kerry Wood (233 in 1998 and 266 in 2003), Mark Prior (245 in 2003), Jake Arrieta (236 in 2015), and Yu Darvish (229 in 2019).

GAME

33. Milt Pappas came within one pitch of a perfect game against the Padres September 2, 1972. With a 3-2 count on Larry Stahl with two out in the ninth, plate umpire Bruce Froemming called a close pitch ball four. Pappas, fuming, retired the next hitter on a pop-up to second baseman Carmen Fanzone to complete his no-hitter. Until the day he died in 2016, Pappas would tell you—and he told me in 2007 when I met him!—that the pitch was a strike.

34. Besides Milt Pappas, the following four Cubs threw seven perfect innings. All four allowed the first batter in the eighth to reach:

Jack Taylor, double vs. Boston on June 11, 1902. He lost the game, 3–2, on a two-run walk-off double.

Glen Hobbie, home run vs. Cincinnati on July 20, 1960. He pitched a two-hitter, giving up a two-out single in the ninth.

Jose Guzman, walk vs. Atlanta on April 6, 1993. He lost a no-hitter on a two-out single in the ninth.

Drew Smyly, single vs. Los Angeles on April 21, 2023. Smyly and catcher Yan Gomes collided going after David Peralta's dribbler, which went for a single. Smyly recorded the next two outs and departed, having struck out 11. The Cubs won the game, 13–0.

35. Jack Pfiester struck out 17 Cardinals in the first game of a doubleheader, on May 30, 1906. This is a bit of a trick question, as that game went 15 innings.

36. Kerry Wood followed up his 20-K game later that year by striking out 16 Reds at Cincinnati on August 26, 1998. The only other Cub to strike out 16 batters is Mark Prior, who did it twice (June 26, 2003 vs. Brewers and September 30, 2004 vs. Reds).

37. Before Kerry Wood's 20-K game, the most strikeouts in a nine-inning game by a Cub was 15, held by three pitchers:

Dick Drott vs. Braves, May 26, 1957 (first game)

Burt Hooton vs. Mets, September 15, 1971 (first game—this was Hooton's second MLB start)

Rick Sutcliffe vs. Phillies, September 3, 1984

Two others struck out 15 in extra-inning games.

Tom Hughes vs. Reds, July 31, 1901, 14 innings

Grover Alexander vs. Phillies, August 2, 1919, 14 innings

38. Don Cardwell threw a no-hitter against the Cardinals May 15, 1960, in the second game of a doubleheader, his first game with the Cubs after being acquired in a trade two days earlier from the Phillies along with first baseman Ed Bouchee for Cal Neeman and Tony Taylor. Cardwell allowed just one baserunner, a walk to Alex Grammas in the second inning. The no-hitter was preserved by a running catch of a sinking liner to left by left fielder Walt "Moose" Moryn. This remains the only no-hitter in MLB history by a pitcher in his first game with a team.

39. Ken Holtzman and Jake Arrieta are the two pitchers who threw two no-hitters for the Cubs in the Modern Era.

Holtzman no-hit the Braves on August 19, 1969, at Wrigley Field. This no-hitter is notable for being one of just two in MLB history with no strikeouts.

Holtzman then no-hit the Reds on June 3, 1971, in Cincinnati. The Cubs won the game 1–0 and Holtzman also scored the only run of the game, reaching base on an error, advancing to second on a groundout and scoring on a single by Glenn Beckert.

Arrieta no-hit the Dodgers on August 30, 2015, in Los Angeles. It was part of a second half in which Arrieta posted an ERA of 0.75 and WHIP of 0.727 in 15 starts. During that span he hit as many home runs (two) as he allowed.

Arrieta no-hit the Reds on April 21, 2016, in Cincinnati. It was his second no-hitter in a span of 11 regular season starts. The Cubs won, 16–0, which is the biggest score of any no-hitter in MLB history.

40. The last Cub to throw a complete game no-hitter at Wrigley Field is Milt Pappas, who did it on September 2, 1972.

Fifty-two years and two days later, September 4, 2024, three pitchers, Shōta Imanaga, Nate Pearson, and Porter Hodge, combined on a no-hitter against the Pirates. The Cubs won the game, 12–0. Imanaga threw seven innings, striking out seven. Pearson and Hodge threw the eighth and ninth, respectively. It was the second combined no-hitter in Cubs history; they also threw one against the Dodgers in Los Angeles on June 24, 2021 (Zach Davies, Ryan Tepera, Andrew Chafin, and Craig Kimbrel).

41. Carlos Zambrano no-hit the Astros on September 14, 2008, at Miller Park in Milwaukee. The game had been moved there due to Hurricane Ike, which had prompted evacuations in the Houston area. Most of the crowd—including this writer—were Cubs fans who had driven up from Chicago, so the 23,441 in attendance were roaring as Big Z struck out Darin Erstad to end the game. He had allowed just one baserunner, hitting Hunter Pence with a pitch with two out in the fifth.

The Cubs nearly duplicated the feat the next afternoon in the second game of the series moved from Houston to Milwaukee. Ted Lilly threw six no-hit innings before allowing a single in the seventh. The Astros scored a run without a hit off Jeff Samardzija and Carlos Marmol in the eighth, but the Cubs won 6–1 with that seventh-inning single being the only Astros hit.

The one hit allowed by the Cubs in the two games remains the only time in MLB history a team has allowed just one hit in consecutive games.

42. Lefty Tyler threw a 21-inning complete game at home vs. the Phillies on July 17, 1918. He allowed one run on 13 hits, walked one, and struck out eight, facing 77 batters. Ed Reulbach pitched 20 innings at Philadelphia on August 24, 1905. He also allowed 13 hits but walked four, hit a batter, and had seven strikeouts. The Cubs won both games by the identical score: 2–1.

43. After Cubs starter Bert Humphries retired the first two batters at home vs. the Dodgers on June 17, 1915, he allowed three straight hits, scoring one run. Right-hander George Washington "Zip" Zabel took over and pitched in relief for 18.1 innings. During that long relief outing, he allowed two runs on nine hits, walked one (intentionally), and struck out six, facing 63 batters. The Cubs had tied the game, 3–3, on a one-out homer in the 15th inning by Vic Saier, and won it in the 19th, 4–3, when a two-out throwing error by the second baseman let a runner score from second. The time of this game: just three hours, thirty minutes!

MANAGERS

QUESTIONS

1. Of the 14 Cubs managers who managed for at least 500 games, who won the most games? Who had the highest winning percentage?
Answer on page 83.

2. Name the four Cubs managers who managed at least 1,000 games.
Answer on page 83.

3. Who was the last manager of the Cubs for at least five seasons? Who was the next to last?
Answer on page 84.

4. Who was the last manager of the Cubs for more than five seasons?
Answer on page 85.

5. Name the managers of the Cubs when they won National League pennants in the Modern Era.
Answer on page 85.

6. Name two managers who took over during the season and led the Cubs to first-place finishes.
Answer on page 87.

7. Name the managers who guided the Cubs to first-place finishes in their first full seasons as manager.
Answer on page 87.

8. Who was the manager of the Cubs in their first season, 1871?
Answer on page 88.

9. Who was the manager of the Cubs in the first season of the National League, 1876?
Answer on page 88.

10. Who was the manager of the Cubs in the first season of the Modern Era, 1901?
Answer on page 89.

11. Which Cubs manager had to step down during a season because of ill health?
Answer on page 89.

12. Which Cubs manager was fired while in the hospital for brain surgery?
Answer on page 90.

13. Which Cubs manager was fired with four games left in a season?
Answer on page 90.

14. Which Cubs manager quit with seven games left in a season?
Answer on page 90.

15. Which Cubs manager was fired 10 games into a season?
Answer on page 91.

16. Which Cubs manager later managed a team that twice swept the Cubs in the World Series?
Answer on page 92.

17. Who managed the Cubs for an entire season that lasted only 113 games?
Answer on page 92.

18. Who was the last Cubs manager who started a season and did not complete it?
Answer on page 93.

19. Who had three tenures as manager of the Cubs?
Answer on page 93.

20. Who was the last player-manager of the Cubs, appearing in 27 games, all as a pinch-hitter?
Answer on page 94.

21. Who was the last player-manager of the Cubs who played in the field, appearing in 13 games?
Answer on page 95.

22. Who was the last player-manager of the Cubs who played in the field in at least half of the team's games?
Answer on page 95.

23. Who was the last player-manager of the Cubs at a position other than first base?
Answer on page 96.

24. In 1961, the Cubs began their ill-conceived College of Coaches to replace the manager. Who was the first head coach of the Cubs under this system?
Answer on page 96.

25. Who "head coached" the most games under the College of Coaches?
Answer on page 97.

26. Which Cubs manager operated an orange grove in California?
Answer on page 97.

27. Which Cubs manager was a longtime umpire both before after serving as skipper of the Cubs?
Answer on page 98.

28. In 1925, for the only time, the Cubs had three full-time managers. Who were they?
Answer on page 99.

29. Twice, the Cubs changed managers during a season and went on to win the pennant. What were the seasons and who were the managers?
Answer on page 99.

30. The "College of Coaches" was the Cubs' ill-considered experiment in 1961–62 of having multiple managers during the course of the seasons. Which of the part-time skippers later served as full-time manager for the final two thirds of a season?
Answer on page 100.

31. Which Cubs manager left the team during a game, saying he was ill, but secretly went to his twelve-year-old stepson's summer camp in Wisconsin?
Answer on page 100.

32. Which Cubs manager made an extended, expletive-packed rant about the team's fans?
Answer on page 101.

33. Which two Cubs managers also managed the White Sox?
Answer on page 101.

34. Three Cubs managers subsequently became the team's general manager. Who were they?
Answer on page 101.

35. Among the 30 full-time Cubs managers for at least 300 regular-season games in the Modern Era, six were primarily catchers during their playing days. Name as many as you can.
Answer on page 102.

36. Four were primarily first basemen during their playing days. Name as many as you can.
Answer on page 102.

37. Nine primarily played second, third, or shortstop during their playing days. Name as many as you can.
Answer on page 102.

38. Four primarily played outfield during their playing days. Name as many as you can.
Answer on page 102.

39. One primarily was a pitcher in his playing days. Name this Cubs manager.
Answer on page 102.

40. One played almost an equal number of games at first base (771) and in the outfield (752). Name this Cubs manager.
Answer on page 102.

41. Five never played in the major leagues. Name as many as you can.
Answer on page 103.

MANAGERS

ANSWERS

1. The Cubs manager with the most wins is Adrian "Cap" Anson, who managed the club for its first 62 games of 1879 and then from 1880–97, 19 seasons in all, with 1,282 wins and 932 losses. The team won five National League pennants under his leadership. He was a player, too, for all 19 of those seasons, in an era when one man could easily do both jobs, and in many cases was expected to. It was a very different time.

In addition to being the winningest manager in Cubs history, he also stands as one of the greatest players in franchise history, with 3,012 hits with the team (1876–97).

2. While Anson had the most wins as Cubs manager, his winning percentage of .579 stands second in franchise history to Frank Chance. Chance took over as manager in 1905 when Frank Selee had to resign due to illness, and immediately led the team to four pennants in five years. Overall, Chance registered 768 wins and just 389 losses as Cubs manager for a .664 winning percentage. As was the case with Anson, Chance was also a player for all of his Cubs seasons, though he became a part-time player after 1908.

His playing numbers are as impressive as his managing totals. In 1903 he stole a MLB-leading 67 bases, which remains the

Cubs franchise record, and also led the majors with 57 in 1906, when the Cubs won 116 games, a record that still stands.

Chance was elected to the Hall of Fame along with his teammates Johnny Evers and Joe Tinker in 1946.

In addition to Chance and Anson, two other Cubs managers led the team for over 1,000 games: Charlie Grimm and Leo Durocher.

Grimm had two long stints as Cubs manager, first from 1932–38. In that first stint he replaced Rogers Hornsby in mid-1932 after players lodged multiple complaints about Hornsby's irascible managing style, and Grimm led the Cubs to the pennant. That was reversed in 1938 when Grimm was replaced by Gabby Hartnett, who helped manage the team to the league title that year.

Grimm returned to manage the Cubs from 1944–49, winning the NL pennant in 1945 but then presiding over a long period of decline. Team owner P. K. Wrigley brought Grimm out of the radio booth for one last managing job with the Cubs in 1960. That lasted 17 games before Grimm returned to radio and Lou Boudreau came out of the booth to manage the team the rest of that year.

Durocher was hired in October 1965 after the failure of the ill-conceived "College of Coaches." In his introductory press conference, Durocher famously said, "If nothing has been said about my title yet, I am not a 'head coach.' I'm the manager."

Durocher did lead the Cubs to several winning seasons after they had been near the bottom of the league for two decades, but failed to win a division title or pennant. He was fired in July 1972.

3. The last two men to manage the Cubs for five seasons were Jim Riggleman (1995–99) and Joe Maddon (2015–19).

Riggleman had been an unsuccessful manager of the Padres

for three years (.385 winning percentage) before the Cubs hired him. He immediately led them to a winning season (73–71) in which they were still contending for a playoff spot in the season's final weekend. Two losing years followed, but then Sammy Sosa's MVP season helped Riggleman manage the team to a wild card spot in 1998.

Hopes were high for a repeat in 1999, but after a good 32–23 start, the team had the worst record in MLB the rest of the year at 35–72 and there were reports that Cubs players had quit on Riggleman, who was fired at the end of the year.

Maddon was brought in unexpectedly when he exercised an opt-out in his contract that became available when Rays general manager Andrew Friedman departed for the Dodgers. Theo Epstein jumped on the opportunity, hiring Maddon and firing Rick Renteria, who had a year left on his contract. In Maddon's introductory news conference, he said he was "talking playoffs, this year," and meant it, and the Cubs exploded for a 97-win season and made the NLCS.

Maddon's leadership style was at least partly responsible for the Cubs finally breaking their 108-year World Series drought and winning in 2016, though he was also criticized for some of his bullpen use during the Series. Two more postseason years followed, but no more titles, and after the Cubs collapsed in September 2019, Maddon's contract expired and was not renewed.

4. Leo Durocher, who managed the Cubs from 1966 until 1972, when he was let go after 90 games (and a 46–44 record).

5. In addition to Chance, Grimm and Maddon, the three other men who managed the Cubs to NL pennants in the Modern Era are Fred Mitchell, Joe McCarthy and Gabby Hartnett.

Mitchell's single pennant was a bit of a fluke. He had been coaching the Braves under George Stallings, and reports were that the Cubs wanted to hire Stallings away from Boston, but they wouldn't let him go, so the Cubs "settled" for Mitchell.

In 1918, the baseball season was ended in early September because of World War I after about 130 games. The Cubs had a 10 1/2 game lead at the time and were declared pennant winners, but lost to the Red Sox in the World Series. Mitchell managed the Cubs for three more seasons, never again coming close to a pennant, then returned to the Braves to manage them for three years, two of which wound up as 100-loss seasons. He coached baseball at Harvard for many years after that.

The end of McCarthy's tenure stands as one of the worst mistakes ever made by the Cubs. Hired away from a minor-league team in Louisville in 1926, McCarthy immediately turned the Cubs into a contender, and they won the NL pennant in 1929, their first in 11 years.

They also led the league for much of 1930, but fell out of first place in September largely because of a great run by the Cardinals, who finished 17–4 while the Cubs went 10–9.

Team owner William Wrigley was incensed, feeling the Cubs should have won two straight pennants, and fired McCarthy with four games remaining in the season. McCarthy went on to manage the Yankees for 16 seasons, winning eight pennants and seven World Series. Would he have done that in Chicago? Obviously we'll never know, but perhaps the Cubs of the 1930s would have won more pennants than they did if McCarthy had stayed.

Hartnett replaced Grimm halfway through the 1938 season and led them to the pennant, including his own famous Homer in the Gloamin' that won a key September game against the Pirates. But Hartnett, perhaps not really fit to be a manager, had a fourth-place finish in 1939 and a losing season in 1940, after which he was fired. He never managed again.

6. Grimm and Hartnett both took over Cubs teams midseason and guided them to the NL pennant.

In 1932, Rogers Hornsby had pretty much alienated all the Cubs players, as well as team president William Veeck, who nearly resigned when William Wrigley hired Hornsby over his objection.Veeck stayed when Wrigley promised not to interfere again. Hornsby had what his SABR biography termed a "reign of terror" before Veeck fired him in early August with the team five games out of first. Grimm led them to a 37–18 record and the pennant.

But Grimm's leadership had worn thin by 1938, and the team was 4.5 games out of first place when he was fired and replaced by Hartnett. The Cubs went 44–27 under Hartnett and won the pennant.

7. Jim Frey was one of the best managerial hires in Cubs history. He took over a team that had lost 91 games the year before and led them to 96 wins, their most since 1945, and the NL East title.

It didn't hurt that just before the season began, general manager Dallas Green had traded for Gary Matthews and Bob Dernier, who were two of the key catalysts for the team, and added Rick Sutcliffe by trade in June.

And Frey helped Ryne Sandberg tweak his swing to drive the ball more, and Sandberg was named National League MVP.

Frey couldn't duplicate his great 1984 season and was fired by mid-1986.

Dusty Baker had the same path as Cubs manager. He was hired off a 95-win, pennant-winning season for the Giants in 2002, and felt like a breath of fresh air as the Cubs won 88 games and the NL Central title. But a collapse down the stretch in 2004 left the team out of the postseason, and Baker, who had a reputation as a players' manager, let some players run the clubhouse, to the detriment of team unity. Baker remained for two more losing seasons before his contract expired and was not renewed.

Piniella, too, had come from success (World Series for the Reds in 1990, several postseason appearances for the Mariners) and was seen as an outsider who could shake things up. He took a 96-loss 2006 team and got them division titles in 2007 with 85 wins and 97 wins in 2008.That second division title had them as World Series favorites. But they got swept by the Dodgers in a Division Series and Piniella seemed to lose interest after that, eventually retiring in August 2010.

8. Jimmy Wood was a player-manager in the early days of the National Association of Base Ball (yes, two words!) Players, the proto-league that predated the National League.

A second baseman, he managed the first iteration of the franchise that would eventually become the Cubs. They played just 28 games in 1871, going 19–9. The team went on hiatus for two years because of the Great Chicago Fire of October 1871, and Wood managed the reconstituted Chicago team again in 1874 and 1875. But in 1876, when the Chicago team was reorganized into the franchise that is now the Cubs, Wood became a National League umpire instead of managing. He umpired just a handful of games before leaving the sport and going on to invest in the citrus industry in Florida. Later his daughter Carrie married William Chase Temple, a citrus baron who created the Temple Cup, given to National League champions in the 1890s. Wood died in San Francisco in 1927.

9. Albert Spalding was both a pitcher and manager for the 1876 Chicago White Stockings, the team that eventually became known as the Cubs.

Leaving field play and managing after 1877, Spalding eventually became team president and led the franchise through a golden age in the 1880s, when they won five NL pennants. In the winter of 1888–89 he led the team on a world tour that exposed baseball to people in Australia, New Zealand, Ceylon, Egypt, Italy, France and England.

While all this was going on, Spalding also opened a sporting-goods store in Chicago that eventually morphed into the manufacture of all sorts of sports-related goods, a company that exists to this day. Spalding himself retired from the business in 1902 and died in 1915.

10. Tom Loftus had taken over as Chicago NL manager in 1899 and thus was their first manager in what we now know as the "Modern Era" of baseball, beginning in 1901. Loftus had previously managed NL teams in Cleveland and Cincinnati, as well as being a manager in Milwaukee in the briefly-major-league Union Association in 1884 and for the Cleveland American Association team in 1889.

His two years in Chicago weren't successful and after 1902 he departed for the upstart American League's Washington Senators, where he managed there for two seasons before departing baseball

11. Frank Selee was hired away from the Boston Braves to manage the Cubs in 1902. He had been responsible for winning six pennants in Boston and was seen by Cubs ownership as the man who could help lead the team back to the success they'd had in the nineteenth century.

The team was in first place for much of 1903 before finishing third and then won 93 games in 1904, though finishing a distant second behind the Giants. In 1905, Selee's team was in fourth place with a 37–28 record when he stepped down due to ill health. He died of tuberculosis in 1909, aged just 49.

12. Frank Chance had been Cubs manager for eight seasons by 1912. They had won four pennants and finished second two other times. After the 1912 season he was hospitalized for blood clots that had, in part, been caused by multiple times he'd been hit by pitches in the head. Team owner Charles Murphy had been selling off players to try to save money, and when the Yankees approached him for Chance's services, Murphy let Chance go as a player and manager while Chance was still in the hospital.

Chance recovered and managed the Yankees in 1913 and 1914. The team wasn't very good either year and Chance resigned to return to his native California to run an orange grove. He later managed the Red Sox in 1923 and had signed to manage the White Sox but could not take the position because ill health had returned. He died in 1924, aged just 48.

13. Joe McCarthy had the unfortunate fate of being the Cubs manager when they were in a late-season pennant race with the Cardinals in 1930. While the Cubs had a decent finish, the Cardinals went 17–4 over their last 21 games. Almost no team could catch up with that, but team owner William Wrigley blamed McCarthy for the Cubs not winning a second straight pennant, and dismissed him with four games remaining in the season. The Cubs trailed by 2 1/2 games and still had a chance to win the pennant, and did in fact win all four games under new manager Rogers Hornsby. But the Cardinals went 4–1 over that span and won the pennant by two games.

14. Herman Franks had the Cubs in contention in 1977 and 1978 with teams that, quite honestly, weren't even close to being that good. They managed to remain in contention through most of 1979 with another team that wasn't very good. The '79 Cubs were 67–54 and four games out of first place after defeating the Dodgers on August 20. But they then went on an 11–23 skid and with a week to go in the season, Franks told the Associated Press that some of his players were "crazy." Newspapers couldn't wait to get that in print, and most Cubs simply rolled their eyes while Franks told the AP's Joe Mooshil that he had intended the remark in confidence.

While Franks had intended to retire after the 1979 season—unless, he said, he could see a 1980 contender, which wasn't likely to happen—he realized he couldn't stay, nor did he want to, after those comments became public. And so, on the morning of September 24, he resigned. Longtime coach Joe Amalfitano took the reins on an interim basis and went 2–5 the rest of the way. Amalfitano managed the Cubs again in 1980 after Preston Gomez was fired and through continued to lead the club through the strike-shortened 1981 season.

15. Jimmie Wilson had managed the Phillies for five of their worst seasons in the 1930s, losing 100 games twice and posting an overall .370 winning percentage.

This didn't stop the Cubs from hiring him in 1941. Perhaps predictably, the Cubs put up three pretty bad years—the first time they'd had three straight losing seasons in 40 years, since 1900–02.

And so, when the team got off to a 1–9 start in 1944, Wilson was fired. Coach Roy Johnson replaced him for a game, then Charlie Grimm was brought back to the manager's chair and actually posted an over .500 record at 74–69, perhaps presaging the 1945 NL pennant-winning Cubs.

That 1–9 start was one win, followed by nine losses. The nine-game losing streak reached 13, which remained the franchise record until the 1997 team started the year 0–14.

Wilson had been a pretty good catcher during his playing career, making two All-Star teams and was pressed into service at age 39 while a coach for the Reds in 1940. He wound up going

6-for-17 and had a key hit (and stolen base!) in Game Seven of the World Series that year, which the Reds won.

Too bad that didn't translate into a good managing career.

16. Joe McCarthy had managed the Cubs for four seasons, winning the 1929 pennant but falling short of a World Series win.

Team owner William Wrigley, upset that the Cubs were going to fall short of repeating as league champions in 1930, fired McCarthy with four games remaining in the season.

He would go on to manage the Yankees to eight pennants and seven World Series titles. Two of those were over the Cubs, both four-game sweeps, in 1932 and 1938. The Cubs were thoroughly outclassed in those eight games, outscored 59–28.

Would they have done better under McCarthy? It's impossible to know, of course, but firing him when he had helped the Cubs come out of their early-1920s doldrums was one of the biggest mistakes in franchise history.

17. Tom Trebelhorn, who had managed the Milwaukee Brewers for six years, four of them winning seasons, was hired to manage the Cubs in 1994.

The team got off to a 3–9 start and lost their first 12 home games. After the ninth of those losses, 6–5 to the Rockies on April 29, Trebelhorn kept a promise he had made during the previous road trip to "talk to fans" if the team lost another home game, and so Trebelhorn dressed after the game in "jeans, a Cubs turtleneck and a beer-company baseball cap," according to the *Chicago Tribune*, and went out to meet fans in front of the firehouse that sits across from Wrigley Field on Waveland Avenue.

As it turned out, it was probably the best thing Trebelhorn ever did as manager of the Cubs. Calmly and slowly, he answered fans' questions and won them over. One fan, quoted in the *Tribune*, said, "First, I appreciate you coming here because I think it takes a lot of guts."

The team did a bit better after the bad start got to 11–24. From then through August 1, they posted a 37–32 record—not too bad—but then lost eight of nine. After that a players' strike ended the season.

Trebelhorn was not asked back and never managed in the big leagues again, though he was a coach for the Orioles for several years in the early 2000s. Cubs fans, though, will always remember the "firehouse chat."

18. Lou Piniella, who began managing the Cubs in 2007, was the most recent team manager to begin a season and not complete it.

Piniella's leadership helped the Cubs win division titles in 2007 and 2008 (and he was named NL Manager of the Year in '08), but the 2009 team fell several games short. That wasn't really Piniella's fault; it was more the presence of Milton Bradley, a divisive influence, and at times Lou seemed to be disconnected from the team.

That feeling continued into the early parts of 2010, with the team dropping under .500 early and never really recovering. On July 27 they began a long stretch of losing, going 5–19 through a win August 19 over the Braves. After that game, Piniella announced he'd be retiring following the next day's game, saying that he wanted to return to his native Tampa to help look after his elderly mother.

While that was certainly true, it appeared that Piniella had just had enough of managing. The Cubs might have reinforced that message by losing his final game as a manager to the Braves 16–5.

19. Charlie Grimm managed the Cubs for three separate stints: 1932–38, 1944–49, and 1960.

The first stint included two pennants, but he was replaced

during the 1938 season and Gabby Hartnett finished off that pennant-winning year. Grimm was at the helm again during the 1945 pennant season, but the team fell into disrepair, and he left after 1949, going on to manage the Braves in Boston and Milwaukee for several years—but was fired a year before the Braves won two straight pennants in 1957 and 1958.

The 1960 stint was odd, and abbreviated. The Cubs fired Bob Scheffing after 1959, despite two pretty good years, and brought Grimm out of retirement to lead the team in 1960, at age 61. Just three other men who managed in 1960 (Charlie Dressen, Jimmie Dykes and Casey Stengel) were older.

Things quickly turned bad for Grimm, and he was replaced after just 17 games in which the team went 6–11. Lou Boudreau was brought out of the WGN radio booth to manage. This wasn't necessarily a bad idea, as Boudreau had been a successful manager in Cleveland and Boston and was just 42. Grimm took Boudreau's spot in the radio booth.

Neither move worked. Grimm was out of place on the radio and the Cubs finished 60–94, so after the season Boudreau went back to the booth and Grimm became a special advisor to team owner P. K. Wrigley.

20. Phil Cavarretta was the most recent player-manager of the Cubs.

A great player for the team who played for them in three World Series (1935, 1938, and 1945), Cavarretta became player-manager in 1951, replacing Frank Frisch. The team did reasonably well under him in 1952, finishing at .500, which would be their last non-losing season until 1963. A lot of that success was due to Hank Sauer's MVP season that year.

The Cubs declined again in 1953 and when Cavarretta was asked how the team would do in 1954, he told the truth: That they would be a "second-division" team. "Second-division" was a common phrase used before divisional play to denote a team finishing in the bottom half of the standings.

Team owner P. K. Wrigley didn't like hearing that and fired Cavarretta before Opening Day. He caught on with the White Sox and played as a part-timer there for two seasons before retiring.

Cavarretta had been scheduled to have his number (44) retired by the Cubs in early 1954 but when he was fired, that ceremony was cancelled and no Cub had a number retired while the Wrigleys still owned the team. Nevertheless, clubhouse manager Yosh Kawano kept No. 44 out of circulation for many years. When Burt Hooton joined the team in 1971 and wanted that number, as he had worn it in college, Yosh had him call Cavarretta for permission.

21. Cavarretta was also the last Cubs player-manager to play in the field, playing 13 games at first base for the team in 1952.

The Chicago native, who attended Lane Tech High School, stayed in baseball for many years after retiring, managing minor-league teams in the Tigers, Athletics, and Indians systems and one season with a Cubs minor-league club in Lancaster, California in 1961. He was also a major-league coach for a while with the Tigers and Mets.

22. The last Cubs player-manager who played at least half of his team's games in the field was Charlie Grimm, who played 104 games at first base in 1933.

Grimm continued to play some games in the field for the next three seasons, but the number of games declined and by 1937 he completely stopped playing in the field.

Grimm was a much better player than many give him credit for. In 1925 he batted .306/.354/.439 and received some down ballot MVP votes, also receiving MVP votes in 1930 and 1932.

He finished his career with 2,299 hits, and that combined with his 1,287 wins as a manager (along with three NL pennants) could eventually get him Hall of Fame consideration by one of the Hall's Era Committees.

23. Rogers Hornsby was the last Cubs player-manager to play a position other than first base, when he played six games at third base and 10 in the outfield in 1932. That was also the year Hornsby was fired as manager after alienating pretty much everyone on the team, as well as management.

Hornsby was hired at the end of 1930 when Joe McCarthy was ill-advisedly let go by team owner William Wrigley. According to Peter Golenbock's Cubs history *Wrigleyville*, Hornsby was so disliked that when a firecracker went off in the stands, Woody English, who actually liked Hornsby, remembered thinking that somebody must have just shot Hornsby.

He was fired mid-1932 and replaced by Grimm, who led the Cubs to the NL pennant.

24. The first "head coach" of the ill-fated Cubs College of Coaches was Vedie Himsl.

A Minnesota native, Himsl had pitched in eight minor-league seasons stretching from 1939–51, with interruptions for World War II service and some years managing in the Cardinals minor-league system.

The Cubs hired Himsl as a scout in 1952 and two years later he became Midwestern scouting director for the team. He managed in the Cubs system in 1957 at their Class D affiliate, Pulaski (Virginia), and the following year he was named pitching instructor for all the Cubs minor-league teams. Just 41 at the time, a coaching future in the Cubs organization for Himsl seemed bright.

Himsl was the first of eight coaches assigned throughout the system to be given the title of "head coach." He "head coached" the first 11 games, with the team going 5–6, before he was shipped off for a stint at Double-A San Antonio and Wenatchee, replaced by Harry Craft. Craft was the head coach for 12 games (4–8) before Himsl returned, which *The Sporting News* headlined on May 17 as good for the club: "Players Hail Himsl's Return to Cubs." The paper noted in a positive way his "strong silent type demeanor." It didn't help, though, as Himsl's 17-game stint resulted in a 5–12 mark. He was replaced again by Tappe (0–2) and Craft (3–1) before Himsl returned again for three games at the top spot (0–3).

He never managed (or "head coached") in the major leagues after 1961, but did serve as Cubs pitching coach in 1962 and 1963. After that he split time managing in the Cubs minor leagues and serving in the Cubs front office until 1968. He was then named director of MLB's Central Scouting Bureau before returning to the Cubs as director of scouting in 1972, a position he kept through 1985.

25. Charlie Metro was the longest-tenured "head coach" under the College of Coaches system, holding the top spot for 112 games in 1962, posting a 42–69 record.

He was also the final man to lead the team under the College of Coaches system, which was ditched after 1962. Bob Kennedy and Lou Klein led the team from 1963–65 with the title of head coach, but there was no rotating system, and those men were essentially managers without the title.

Metro, whose birth name was Charles Moreskonich, later worked as a scout and coach in the White Sox, Tigers and Cardinals systems before a brief 52-game stint as manager of the Royals in 1970.

26. Frank Chance was not only a Cubs manager, he was a businessman outside of baseball. After leaving managing the

Yankees in 1914, he returned to his native California and ran an orange grove in Whittier which, per *The New York Times*, he had purchased in 1910 for $25,000—an amount roughly equal to $800,000 in 2025. That was the second such business Chance had invested in, as he had previously owned such a grove in Glendora.

Chance made quite a bit of money in that industry, but his baseball itch returned and in 1922, he sold off his business interests in California and signed on to manage the Boston Red Sox. His one year at the helm in Boston led to a 61–91 record and the following year he had signed to manage the White Sox, but due to a lingering illness could not take that job. Chance died on September 15, 1924, in Los Angeles.

27. Chicago native Hank O'Day had been a major-league player from 1884–90 and after two years in the minor leagues, unable to play due to injuries but wanting to stay in baseball, took up umpiring in the Northwestern League.

Umpiring in the 1890s was a dangerous profession, as fans did not hesitate to attack umps for calls perceived to go against them. O'Day quit after a couple of years and returned to Chicago to work in the city recorder's office. Baseball called again in an odd way—O'Day was sitting in the stands before a Chicago Colts (predecessor nickname to the Cubs) game and the then-single umpire hadn't shown. Team owner James Hart recognized O'Day and asked him to fill in. He did so well that the National League immediately hired him and he worked as an umpire through 1913. Famously, he was the umpire who ruled the "Merkle Game" in 1908 as a tie game when Fred Merkle failed to touch first base.

In 1914, O'Day was hired to manage the Cubs. They finished a respectable fourth, but O'Day was fired and went back to umpiring in 1915, finally retiring after 1927, having umpired 35 MLB seasons.

28. The three-manager season for the Cubs, the only one in franchise history (with the exceptions of the College of Coaches and a few years where there was an interim manager for one or two games) was 1925, when Bill Killefer, Rabbit Maranville, and George Gibson managed the team.

Killefer had been the team's manager since mid-1921 and they had three decent, though not really contending, seasons from 1922–24. When they got off to a bad start in 1925, Killefer was fired with the team at 33–42 and replaced by Maranville.

This might have been one of the worst decisions in franchise history. Maranville, who had a long career of success with the Braves and Pirates, had been acquired by the Cubs before the 1925 season, already on the down side of that career. Admittedly a heavy drinker, Maranville wasn't an appropriate leader for the team and was let go after just 53 games with a 23–30 record.

The trade that brought Maranville to the Cubs worked out in the end, as a young first baseman named Charlie Grimm also came over from the Pirates in that trade.

George Gibson, a coach with the 1925 Cubs, finished off the year as manager with a 12–14 record and then was dismissed when the Cubs hired Joe McCarthy. Which, of course, could have been the best move in franchise managing history if they'd just kept him.

Gibson managed the Pirates from 1932–34 and, after a few years as a minor-league executive, retired to his farm in Ontario. He died in 1967, aged 86.

29. Two Cubs teams changed managers midseason, and the team went on to win the NL pennant.

In 1932, the much-reviled leadership of Rogers Hornsby was replaced by the more easygoing style of Charlie Grimm. The team was 53–46 when Hornsby was fired, and Grimm led them to a 37–18 record and a pennant win by four games. This has happened at other times in MLB history, notably in 1982 when the Brewers replaced Buck Rodgers with the team floundering in fifth place with a 23–24 record. Harvey Kuenn took over and the Brewers went 72–43 and won the AL pennant.

Grimm's style had apparently worn thin by mid-1938 and he was fired July 19 with the team in third place at 45–36. Gabby Hartnett became player-manager, and the Cubs went 44–27 and took their fourth pennant in a 10-year span.

30. Lou Klein managed the Cubs for the last 106 games of the 1965 season, though he was not officially called the manager. The title of the field leader of the Cubs at the time was still "head coach," even though the College of Coaches had been dumped after 1962.

After playing five MLB seasons for the Cardinals, Indians, and Athletics, Klein joined the Cubs system and served as a player-manager at several different levels of the system from 1955–59. In 1960, he was a coach for the Cubs for part of the season and managed in Double-A for the rest of the year.

The following year, Klein became part of the College of Coaches, and had a brief stint as head coach in each of its two seasons. Then he coached under Bob Kennedy for two and a half years before his 106 games as on-field leader in 1965. Leo Durocher replaced Klein and the title of manager was restored for the 1966 season. Klein then coached and scouted in the Cubs organization until he died of a stroke in 1976, aged just 57.

31. Leo Durocher famously ditched the Cubs for a weekend because he had promised his new wife, Lynne Greenblatt, that he would go to parents' weekend at her son's summer camp in Wisconsin.

Durocher claimed to be ill, but instead boarded a private

plane to northern Wisconsin. The *Chicago Tribune* learned of this and reported Durocher's visit to camp.

In modern baseball this might be a scandal enough to cost a manager his job. In fact, team owner P. K. Wrigley was going to fire Durocher and replace him with Herman Franks, but Franks talked him out of it.

Which is kind of too bad, as Franks had just come off a stint of managing the Giants to four straight 90-plus win seasons. He might have been a good antidote for the rough-and-tough Durocher. Durocher's team collapsed late in 1969, as all Cubs fans know, and Leo managed the team until he was fired midseason in 1972. Franks eventually became Cubs manager for three seasons, from 1977–79.

32. Lee Elia's famous rant, recorded by local radio reporter Les Grobstein, came after the Cubs had blown a late-inning lead and fallen to 5–14 on the season.

Elia, frustrated at the loss and because some fans had tried to get onto the field after Keith Moreland, launched into a profane tirade that accused Cubs fans of not having jobs and just coming to Wrigley Field to "boo my players."

General manager Dallas Green thought about firing Elia after that, but ultimately didn't, and Elia lost his job the following year for unrelated reasons. Later, Elia apologized for the tirade and managed and coached with the Phillies for a time, and also spent many years in the Mariners organization.

33. Johnny Evers and Rick Renteria. Both managed the Cubs first: Evers in 1913 and 1921, then the Sox in 1924; Renteria in 2014, then the Sox from 2017–20.

34. Bob Kennedy (1963–65, 182–198 record), Herman Franks (1977–79, 238–241 record), and Jim Frey (1984–86, 196–182 record).

35. Gabby Hartnett, Herman Franks, Bill Killefer, David Ross, Bob Scheffing, and Jimmie Wilson are the Cubs managers who were primarily catchers in their playing days in the major leagues.

In addition, Joe Maddon had a 170-game minor-league playing career before getting into coaching and managing, 129 of those games as a catcher.

36. The Cubs managers who were primarily first basemen were Cap Anson, Phil Cavarretta, Frank Chance, Charlie Grimm, and Jim Marshall, though Marshall also played some games in the outfield. Dusty Baker also played some games at first base late in his career.

37. The Cubs managers whose primary playing position was second base, third base or shortstop were Tom Burns, Craig Counsell, Leo Durocher, Frankie Frisch, Stan Hack, Jim Lefebvre, Dale Sveum, and Don Zimmer.

38. Four Cubs managers were primarily outfielders in their playing days: Dusty Baker, Don Baylor, Bob Kennedy, and Lou Piniella. Phil Cavarretta, primarily a first baseman, also played several hundred games in the outfield during his playing career.

39. Just one Cubs manager in the Modern Era was primarily a pitcher: Fred Mitchell, who managed the Cubs from 1917–20, pitched in the major leagues for five seasons with the Red Sox, Braves, Athletics, and Phillies. Before 1900, the first Cubs manager after the NL formed in 1876, Albert Spalding, was a pitcher.

40. The Cubs manager who split his playing time almost equally between first base and the outfield was Whitey Lockman, who managed the Cubs from the second half of 1972, when he replaced Leo Durocher, through the 1974 season.

Lockman played 15 MLB seasons, 13 of them with the Giants. During that time, he played for Durocher-managed teams in eight of those years, all with the Giants. After his playing career he became a coach, first for the Reds, then the Giants. Following that coaching stint, Lockman joined the Cubs organization as a minor-league manager, coach, and eventually director of player development before being named manager. After he was fired as manager, he continued in various roles in the Cubs front office through 1989.

41. The five Cubs managers who never played in the major leagues were Jim Frey, Joe Maddon, Joe McCarthy, Jim Riggleman, and Frank Selee.

Selee came from a different time. He began in baseball as in investor, putting money into a minor-league team in Waltham, Massachusetts. After running a couple of other local teams in Massachusetts, Selee was hired by teams in higher leagues and became known for identifying and bringing in top talent—much as a scout might do in modern baseball.

Eventually his record came to the attention of the owners of the Boston NL team, who hired him to manage in 1890. Previous playing experience wasn't really needed in those days, as the role of manager was far different than it is today.

Selee managed 12 seasons in Boston and won six NL pennants. The team started to decline about the turn of the twentieth century and Selee was fired after 1901. He was immediately hired by Cubs general manager James Hart, who had been replaced by Selee in Boston in 1890.

The Cubs franchise was in a similar doldrum to what had happened in Boston, but Selee turned things around after one year near .500. In 1903 the Cubs contended for much of the year and finished 82–56, and the following year they won 93 games, then the franchise record.

Selee began the 1905 season as Cubs manager, but health issues forced him to step down in July with the team at 37–28.

Selee was replaced by Frank Chance, who wound up leading the team to four pennants in five years beginning in 1906. Selee died of tuberculosis in 1909, aged just 49.

WRIGLEY FIELD

QUESTIONS

1. How many suspended games were played at Wrigley Field after the National League instituted a rule for such games in 1969?
Answer on page 109.

2. Wrigley Field is the oldest active National League ballpark. What is the second oldest?
Answer on page 110.

3. What was Wrigley Field's previous name?
Answer on page 110.

4. What was its original name?
Answer on page 110.

5. What team was the park built for?
Answer on page 111.

6. What was the name of the Cubs' longtime home park before moving to the North Side?
Answer on page 111.

7. What occupied the land where Wrigley Field stands before it was turned into a ballpark?
Answer on page 111.

8. Name the streets that enclose Wrigley Field.
Answer on page 112.

9. What is the best-known nickname of Wrigley Field?
Answer on page 112.

10. What happened at Wrigley Field on May 2, 1917?
Answer on page 112.

11. What happened at Wrigley Field on October 1, 1932?
Answer on page 113.

12. What happened at Wrigley Field? on September 28, 1938?
Answer on page 113.

13. What was the seating capacity of Wrigley Field when it was built?
Answer on page 114.

14. What is its current capacity?
Answer on page 114.

15. Where does its current capacity rank among active major-league ballparks?
Answer on page 115.

16. When was the upper deck added?
Answer on page 115.

17. What year was the iconic center-field scoreboard built?
Answer on page 115.

18. What year was the ivy planted on the outfield walls?
Answer on page 116.

19. When was the clock added atop the scoreboard?
Answer on page 116.

20. What happened at Wrigley Field on April 26, 1941?
Answer on page 116.

21. Name the Cubs organist who played at Wrigley Field for 2,687 games.
Answer on page 117.

22. Name the three players whose home runs nearly hit the center-field scoreboard?
Answer on page 117.

23. What is the distance from home plate down the line to the wall in left field? In right field?
Answer on page 118.

24. What is the height of the wall in the left- and right-field corners?
Answer on page 118.

25. What is the height in front of the bleachers?
Answer on page 118.

26. When were the baskets installed in front of the bleachers?
Answer on page 118.

27. How many flags are on the left-field foul pole? Who do they honor?
Answer on page 119.

28. How many flags are on the right-field foul pole? Who do they honor?
Answer on page 119.

29. The Cubs' first night game at Wrigley Field was scheduled for August 8, 1988—8/8/88—against the Phillies but was rained out in the fourth inning. When was the first official night game at Wrigley?
Answer on page 119.

30. The marquee above the main entrance to Wrigley Field has been red for many, many seasons. What color was it when it was installed in 1934?
Answer on page 120.

WRIGLEY FIELD

ANSWERS

1. It wasn't until 1969 that a game called for darkness at Wrigley Field caused such an uproar that the National League agreed to have all such games suspended. On Sunday, June 22, 1969, the second game of a doubleheader with the Expos was stopped after six innings, with the Cubs behind 5–4. The time of day was 6:25 p.m. There was still plenty of light, according to Cubs players, and Billy Williams was emphatic, quoted in the *Chicago Tribune*: "I wasn't having any trouble seeing the ball," said the usually mild-mannered Williams, who was steaming at the umpires' decision. "I only had trouble hitting it."

Cubs backup catcher Gene Oliver made a comment that turned out to be prescient: "It's a lousy rule in the first place. They ought to suspend these games. That's a sin to call this game when we had nine outs left." Oliver got his wish. The Cubs complained to the National League office, and three days later team owners changed the rule.

Between 1971 and 1988, when the lights installed at Wrigley Field made the issue moot, the Cubs played 22 home games that were suspended for darkness. Despite their 1969 complaints, they might as well have not bothered—the Cubs were 6–14–2 in those games. (The tie games were first, as a result of the 1981 players' strike, and second, because the suspended game result no longer mattered for any playoff positioning.)

2. The second-oldest ballpark in the National League, believe it or not, is Dodger Stadium, which was built nearly 50 years after Wrigley Field, opening in 1962. All of the other "ancient" parks that were built in the period from 1909–16—Crosley Field, Forbes Field, Connie Mack Stadium, Ebbets Field—were torn down in the late 1960s and early 1970s as cities felt building one stadium for football and baseball would be a cost-saver. Those fields turned out to be suitable for neither sport and in the 1990s and early 2000s were all replaced. There are no longer any MLB parks shared by a baseball team and an NFL team. The last such stadium was the Oakland Coliseum, last shared by the A's and Raiders in 2019.

3. After a group headed by William Wrigley bought the Cubs in 1918, the park was renamed Cubs Park in 1920, and in December 1926 named after its team owner, so it has now been Wrigley Field for nearly 100 years. The name is sometimes considered the first "branding" opportunity for a ballpark, but the fact that Wrigley's gum products were popular was just a side benefit. The park was specifically named to honor the owner.

4. Before it was renamed Cubs Park, the ballpark we now know as Wrigley Field was named after a previous team owner, Charlie Weeghman.

Weeghman had been the owner of the Federal League's Chicago Whales (also known as the Chi-Feds) and had the park built in 1914 for them. When the Federal League folded after 1915, two of its league owners were permitted to buy into National League teams as part of the settlement of the lawsuit brought by Federal League owners. Weeghman bought the Cubs and moved them from West Side Grounds, where they had played since 1893, and the park's name was kept until 1918, when Weeghman sold to a group headed by William Wrigley.

5. An attempt at a third major league was made in 1914, when the eight-team Federal League was formed. A team known both as the Chi-Feds and Chicago Whales was the Chicago entry in this league, and in fact, that team won the FL pennant in 1915.

A lawsuit was filed and, with several FL teams teetering on the edge of bankruptcy, the league entered into an agreement with MLB owners, with two FL owners allowed to buy into NL teams. Charlie Weeghman, Whales owner, bought the Cubs, and Phil Ball, owner of the St. Louis Federal League team, bought the Browns.

6. The Cubs weren't always the North Siders. From 1893–1915 they could have been referred to as the West Siders, as they played at a park called West Side Grounds. Home plate was located at the corner of Polk and Lincoln Streets (that version of Lincoln, different from the one on the North Side, is now called Wolcott). The team won four National League pennants and two World Series with West Side Grounds as their home field before moving to the North Side in 1916.

In 2008, a plaque was placed at 912 S. Wood Street, near the UIC medical campus. The plaque is where the clubhouse and flagpole were once located, marking the location of West Side Grounds. The marker stands at that location to this day.

7. The answer to the question can actually be found right near Wrigley Field today, as Seminary Avenue runs north from Waveland Avenue just across from the left field gate.

A seminary stood on the spot now occupied by Wrigley Field. A Lutheran church had been built on the land in 1874 and by 1891 the Chicago Lutheran Theological Seminary was erected on the spot where Cubs fielders now run after baseballs. The seminary wanted more land and so the plot where Wrigley is now was sold in 1909 and that land owner, Charles Havenor, who once wanted to place a minor-league team in Chicago, leased it to Charlie Weeghman in 1913.

In some older photos of Wrigley Field, a large building can be seen beyond left field. That building was part of the seminary property; later it was demolished and residential buildings built.

8. Wrigley Field is bounded by Clark Street, Addison Street, Waveland Avenue, and Sheffield Avenue, the latter two made more famous because home runs often landed on those streets, or at least they did before the construction of the two large video boards and expansion of the bleachers in 2015. The bleacher expansion, in particular, cut way down on the number of home runs reaching the streets. In 2025, for example, only three home runs landed on Waveland, when in some earlier years a few dozen balls would leave the yard.

9. The best-known nickname for Wrigley Field is "The Friendly Confines," bestowed on the ballyard by Hall of Famer Ernie Banks, who always loved to play at home. In fact, Ernie's numbers were far better at Wrigley, as he batted .290/.348/.537 with 290 home runs in 1,285 games at "The Friendly Confines," but just .259/.311/.462 with 222 home runs in 1,243 games on the road.

10. On May 2, 1917, Fred Toney of the Reds and Jim "Hippo" Vaughn both threw nine no-hit innings. The Reds got a hit and run off Vaughn in the 10th and won the game. For quite some time it was known as the "double no-hitter," until Major League Baseball ruled that no-hitters had to be games that were completed with no hits.

It was the last no-hitter thrown by anyone at Wrigley Field for 38 years, until Sam Jones threw one for the Cubs against the

Pirates May 12, 1955, and Toney's no-no was the last one against the Cubs at Wrigley for 48 years, until Jim Maloney threw one, also for the Reds. Maloney's no-no is the most recent complete-game extra-inning no-hitter, and also the no-hitter with the most walks by the no-hit pitcher (10).

11. October 1, 1932 was the date of Game Three of the World Series between the Yankees and Cubs. The Yankees had won the first two games in New York and the Cubs were looking for revenge.

Babe Ruth smashed a three-run homer in the first inning and Lou Gehrig homered in the third, but the Cubs had come back and tied the game 4–4 going into the top of the fifth.

With one out in the fifth, Ruth came to the plate. To this day there's debate on whether Ruth pointed to the Cubs dugout—as they were heckling him—or toward the seats, indicating he was going to hit a home run. Video that surfaced in recent years is inconclusive, but Ruth indeed homered off Charlie Root. After the game Ruth claimed he was just pointing at the dugout to indicate he had "one strike left," but also, knowing some newspapers claimed he had called his shot, said, "It's in the papers, isn't it?"

Root, for his part, claimed he would have put Ruth "on his ass" if he thought Ruth was calling his shot.

In any case, Gehrig followed with his second homer of the game and the Yankees wound up winning 7–5, and won again the next day to sweep the World Series.

12. Cubs catcher Gabby Hartnett, who was also serving as player-manager in 1938, hit a home run that was to become famous as the "Homer in the Gloamin'", a game-winning blast off Mace Brown of the Pittsburgh Pirates.

The "gloamin'" was a play on words on a popular song called

"Roamin' in the Gloamin,'" and referred to how dark it supposedly was when the home run was hit. One famous photo shows Hartnett crossing the plate, surrounded by ushers and fans, with the sky looking dark—but that was mainly due to the flash photography of the time. Another photo of the scene, taken from the third-base side seats, shows plenty of light still available.

Contrary to popular belief, that home run did not win the pennant for the Cubs, as there were still five games remaining in the season. It did put them in first place for the first time since June 7. It would take four more games to clinch the pennant over the Pirates, a win in the first game of a doubleheader in St. Louis on the season's final day.

13. Wrigley Field had only one deck when it was first completed in 1914 and seated just 14,000. Nevertheless, an estimated 21,000 crammed into the place for its first game, April 23, 1914, between the Chi-Feds and the Kansas City Packers.

By 1927, an upper deck had been completed and the capacity was reported as 38,396. The official capacity of the ballpark varied between about 36,000 and 39,000 for several decades, though standing-room crowds often topped 45,000, and for the 1929, 1932, and 1935 World Series, temporary bleachers were erected over the streets on Waveland and Sheffield. The biggest World Series crowd at Wrigley Field was 50,740 for Game One of the 1929 Fall Classic.

14. With the multiple bleacher expansions in 2006 and 2015 and the additions of suites and private clubs, Wrigley Field's capacity is presently 41,649. The largest announced crowd since the 1060 Project, the renovations of Wrigley Field, was completed is 41,424 for a Cubs-Brewers game August 2, 2019. That number is below the official capacity because player family tickets and other freebies aren't included in the announced total.

15. Wrigley Field's current capacity ranks in the middle of the pack of MLB ballparks: 14th, between American Family Field in Milwaukee, 41,900, and Nationals Park in Washington, 41,373. Dodger Stadium is the largest by far, 56,000, and Chase Field in Phoenix is second at 48,330.

16. Wrigley Field's original capacity of 14,000 increased to about 20,000 in the early 1920s when the entire ballpark was shifted slightly to the east. That sounds odd, but indeed, during the 1922–23 offseason, the existing lower grandstand was cut into three pieces. One piece (right field) remained in place, one piece (plate area) was moved toward Clark Street, the remaining piece (left field) was moved northwest to fill in land that had been cleared by the demolition of structures left over from the seminary campus that had preceded Wrigley.

As demand for tickets increased during the 1920s, plans for an upper deck were made, with the original ballpark architect, Zachary Taylor Davis, doing the design. It opened in 1927 and capacity at that time increased to 38,396.

17. As part of a massive renovation of Wrigley Field, the now-iconic scoreboard was built in 1937. That was the same year the current bleacher structure was completed, in an effort by team owner P. K. Wrigley to beautify the ballpark. The scoreboard was first put in use in late September 1937.

The batter number/ball/strike/out numbers appear at a distance to be lights, but they are actually metal "eyelets" that pop in and out when buttons on a box operated in the press box are pushed. If you are seated in the bleachers near the board, you can actually hear this "pop" noise. The box in the press box is operated by Rick Fuhs, who has gotten so good at it that he'll often have the correct ball or strike posted before the umpire even gives a signal. The box is the original one that came with the board nearly 90 years ago.

18. Another part of P. K. Wrigley's beautification plan was to plant ivy to grow up the brick bleacher wall. Wrigley left the choice and planting of the ivy to Bill Veeck Jr.—yes, the same Veeck who later had two stints as the owner of the White Sox. Veeck's father, Bill Veeck Sr., had been Cubs team president from 1919–33.

The junior Veeck did some of the planting himself, and his work survives and thrives to this day. He never stopped being a Cubs fan, even while owning the Sox. After he sold the White Sox to Jerry Reinsdorf in 1981, he spent many afternoons sitting in the center-field bleachers at Wrigley Field, chatting about baseball with anyone who wanted to until his death in 1986.

19. The clock on top of the Wrigley Field scoreboard is, like the board itself, iconic. The Cubs once gave away working battery-operated replicas and it shows up on T-shirts, usually with the time set at 1:20 without any words. That's an "if you know you know" thing, as every Cubs fan is familiar with the day game time of 1:20 p.m.

But that clock was not on the scoreboard when it was originally erected in 1937. Unfortunately, the number of photos of the board in its early years don't allow us to pin down the exact date when the clock was installed, but there is one photo from May 25, 1941, that shows the board without the clock, and it was placed there sometime after that and before the end of the 1941 season.

The clock originally had its colors reversed from that of the board—it was white with dark dots for the hours. The board was a rust color at the time. In 1944 the entire board, and the clock, were painted the current olive-drab color.

20. Organ music was first heard at Wrigley Field April 26, 1941. Ray Nelson played the organ while fans arrived for that afternoon's game against the Cardinals.

The music had to stop at 2:30 (games began at 3:00 in those days) because that's when the radio broadcast began and some of the organ music was covered by ASCAP and the Cubs would have had to pay royalties if the Wrigley music had been heard on the radio.

After a short time the organ, and organist, vanished. There was no further organ music at Wrigley Field until 1967, when the first Lowery organ was installed and Jack Kearney began to entertain fans pregame and eventually during games.

21. Several organists played at Wrigley Field after the organ was brought back full time in 1967. Between then and 1987, those men were Jack Kearney, Frank Pellico, Vance Fothergill, John Henzl, Ed Vodlicka, and Bruce Miles (no relation to the *Daily Herald* Cubs scribe).

Gary Pressy was hired in 1987 and worked 2,687 consecutive games until his retirement at the end of the 2019 season. John Benedeck and Josh Langhoff now share organist duties at Wrigley Field.

22. No one has hit the Wrigley Field scoreboard with a baseball. Three players who came close were Bill Nicholson of the Cubs in 1948, Eddie Mathews of the Braves in 1953, and Roberto Clemente of the Pirates in 1959. Clemente's ball was reported with various distances, the longest being 565 feet, the most accurate probably being 510 feet. It was witnessed by one of the famed Wrigley Field ballhawks, who claimed it bounced "on the corner" at Waveland and Sheffield and then into a gas station which at the time stood on the northeast corner of that intersection.

You'll note that the words "with a baseball" were used as a qualifier above. That's because on April 17, 1951, famed golfer Sam Snead was invited to Wrigley Field and entertained the crowd of 18,211 by hitting golf balls at the board. At least one hit the board and then Snead hit a majestic shot that cleared the board.

23. The left-field wall at Wrigley Field is 355 feet from home plate and the right-field wall 353 feet. You'll note that this makes Wrigley Field a bit asymmetrical, even though it occupies exactly one square city block. The 400-foot sign denoting the farthest distance from home plate to the ivy-covered bleacher wall is slightly to the right of center field.

24. You might think the Wrigley Field outfield wall is all one uniform height—but after the addition of ribbon boards during the 1060 Project, the left- and right-field corners beyond the "well," the curve where bleacher seats used to end before expansion, are 15 feet high.

25. The rest of the bleacher wall, from well to well on each side, stands at 11 feet, six inches high.

26. In the 1960s, as society began to get a bit more freewheeling, some bleacher fans began to play a game of walking on top of the bleacher wall. The prize for winning was a free beer. This got worse in 1969, when the bleachers were filled on many afternoons. Some fans even jumped on the field—not a great idea, as the nearly 12-foot drop is longer than it looks.

So in 1970, the team decided to install "baskets," actually a small fence on the bleacher wall that would prevent jumping on the field. They also put angled concrete on top of the wall to prevent people from walking on it. At first, the baskets were only in the seating area but later, MLB told teams that had such baskets that they had to line the entire outfield walls with them.

The baskets were installed during a Cubs road trip in late April and early May 1970 and the first game played with them was Thursday, May 7, 1970. Then as now, they extend 42 inches past the bleacher wall and, in addition to preventing fans from jumping on the field, they also prevent fan interference with home runs.

Let's dispel one myth before we leave this topic. At one time, ESPN broadcaster Joe Morgan called the basket "Banks Boulevard" and claimed Ernie only got to 500 home runs because it was there. The date of the installation of the basket proves this Morgan statement false. Banks hit only eight of his 512 career homers at Wrigley Field after the basket was installed, and there's video of three of those eight that survives showing those homers went into the seats. Newspaper reports indicate that all of the other five landed in the seats, not in the basket. Thus, Morgan's so-called "Banks Boulevard" was a myth.

27. Three retired number flags hang from the left-field foul pole. They honor Hall of Famers Ernie Banks (No. 14), Ferguson Jenkins (No. 31), and Ron Santo (No. 10). Banks's number was retired in 1982, Santo's in 2003 and Jenkins's in 2009.

28. Four retired number flags hang from the right-field foul pole. They honor Hall of Famers Billy Williams (No. 26), Ryne Sandberg (No. 23), Greg Maddux (No. 31), and Jackie Robinson (No. 42). Williams's number was retired in 1987, Sandberg's in 2005 and Maddux, along with Jenkins, had the number 31 retired in a joint ceremony in 2009. MLB retired No. 42 for all teams to honor Robinson in 1997, but allowed players, coaches, and managers wearing that number to keep it until the end of their careers. The last Cub to wear No. 42 was coach Dan Radison in 1997. The last Cubs player to wear No. 42 was Dave Smith in 1992.

29. Wrigley Field's first scheduled night game on August 8, 1988 against the Phillies had a tremendous thunderstorm blow through before they could play five innings and make the game official. Too bad, because then Ryne Sandberg would have had the first night game home run. That got wiped off the books when it rained.

The first official night game was the next evening, August 9, 1988, with the Mets as the opponent. The Cubs won 6–4, but the honor of hitting the first night game home run went to Mets outfielder Lenny Dykstra. The first Cub to hit a night game home run was Damon Berryhill, who hit a pair on August 22, 1988, against the Astros. Unfortunately, the Cubs lost that game 9–7.

30. The now-iconic red Wrigley Field marquee was painted a color known as Mallard Green when it was installed above the main entrance of the ballpark at Clark and Addison for the 1934 season. The marquee was erected as part of ballpark improvements that included a new public address system. The first game played after the installation was a preseason exhibition game against the Washington Senators, which the Cubs lost 8–3. The *Chicago Tribune* reported that the new PA system "blew up and was out of commission for half the game."

Over time the marquee has been painted green, blue, red and even purple (for a Northwestern football game in 2010). For Cubs games, it has been its current red color since 1965.

BROADCASTERS

QUESTIONS

1. WGN-TV became the iconic TV home of the Cubs for more than 70 years until their broadcasts stopped after 2019. Which other Chicago TV stations also carried local broadcasts of Cubs games?
   Answer on page 125.

2. Which future president once broadcast Cubs games on the radio?
   Answer on page 125.

3. Cubs games were broadcast on WGN radio for many years. What Chicago radio station carried Cubs games for most of the 1940s and 1950s?
   Answer on page 126.

4. What was the famous catchphrase Cubs radio broadcaster Vince Lloyd would say when a Cubs batter hit a home run?
   Answer on page 126.

5. Which Cubs TV broadcaster was better known for doing play-by-play for the Chicago Blackhawks?
Answer on page 126.

6. Which Cubs broadcaster once held the MLB record for most consecutive strikeouts to start a game?
Answer on page 127.

7. In what year were the Cubs involved in the first satellite broadcast to Europe?
Answer on page 127.

8. Who was the broadcaster originally named by WGN-TV to succeed Jack Brickhouse when he retired?
Answer on page 128.

9. How many no-hitters were televised by WGN-TV?
Answer on page 128.

10. In the early days of radio, broadcast rights were often distributed to multiple stations. Which two baseball broadcasting legends broadcast the 1938 World Series for different Chicago stations?
Answer on page 129.

11. Which future Cubs legend recorded his first major-league base hit during Jack Brickhouse's last Wrigley Field TV broadcast in 1981?
Answer on page 129.

12. Which two Cubs broadcasters famously lost it on-air (twice) while reading a ladies' lingerie commercial between innings?
Answer on page 129.

13. Name two Cubs broadcasters who later became broadcasters for the White Sox.
Answer on page 129.

14. Which Cubs broadcaster left the radio booth to manage the team?
Answer on page 130.

15. Which Cubs broadcaster died in an auto accident during spring training?
Answer on page 130.

16. Which Cubs broadcaster delivered the world's most anguished "Ohhhhh . . . nooooo!" when a dropped fly ball with two outs in the ninth let three runs score and the Cubs lost?
Answer on page 131.

17. Which Cubs broadcaster's toupee caught on fire in the press box at Shea Stadium in New York?
Answer on page 131.

18. Who was the first former Cubs player to become a broadcaster for the team?
Answer on page 132.

19. Name the first baseman who played 66 games in one season for the Cubs, then starred in a TV Western for five seasons.
Answer on page 132.

20. Name the first baseman who played 263 games in five seasons for the Cubs and was the son of a well-known host of TV game shows.
Answer on page 133.

21. Name the Cubs catcher who after his playing days appeared on network TV for more than 30 years, as a baseball color commentator, morning talk-show host, daytime game-show host and late-night talk-show guest.
Answer on page 133.

22. Name the Cub who was at one time was the sports anchor for Chicago station WGN's Sunday night newscast.
Answer on page 134.

23. Name the future manager of the Cubs who appeared as himself in multiple TV shows made in Hollywood.
Answer on page 134.

24. Name the Cubs manager who competed on *Dancing with the Stars.*
Answer on page 135.

BROADCASTERS

ANSWERS

1. In fact, the first Cubs game televised wasn't on WGN-TV—it was on WBKB, then Channel 4 (there's no longer a Channel 4 in Chicago, but that's a tale for a different book). That happened April 20, 1946, when that channel took one TV camera to Wrigley Field to carry that year's home opener, which the Cubs lost, 2–0.

In 1948 WGN-TV started its slate of Cubs TV games while WBKB-TV continued, and in 1949 WENR-TV, then the ABC-owned station in Chicago, also televised the full slate of Cubs home games. In the early days of TV, channels often used sports to fill up the many on-air hours where other programming wasn't available.

By 1953, with more national network programming for local Chicago stations, Cubs baseball was left to WGN-TV, where the channel had a slate of games every year through 2019.

2. President Ronald Reagan was the chief executive who, in a previous career as a radio broadcaster, called Cubs games for WHO radio in Des Moines, Iowa, in the 1930s.

Reagan never traveled to Wrigley Field to do these games. Instead, these broadcasts were recreations, often done in that era by stations where such travel was difficult or impossible. Wire services would send play-by-play by "ticker" and announcers would "call" plays based on that. Sometimes there were delays in sending this information and when that happened, announcers would simply have hitters hit "foul balls" until the ticker caught up.

Reagan did help call one Cubs game on TV while he was president. On September 30, 1988, he was in Chicago to address a convention, and on a whim asked to be taken to Wrigley Field, where he joined Harry Caray in the broadcast booth for part of the Cubs-Pirates game that afternoon, which the Cubs lost in 10 innings, 10–9.

3. WGN didn't take over Cubs broadcasts full time until 1957. Before that, from 1945–56, WIND radio was the Cubs' flagship radio station.

4. For much of that era, the Cubs' main radio play-by-play announcer was Bert Wilson, whose catchphrase was, "I don't care who wins as long as it's the Cubs!"

Other broadcasters announcing Cubs games on WIND included Milo Hamilton, who later did some Cubs TV in the 1980s, and Jack Quinlan, who moved to WGN along with the team in 1958.

Many baseball announcers have special home-run calls. For Vince Lloyd, it was yelling out "Holy mackerel!" when a Cubs player hit a home run.

5. Lloyd was the Cubs' play-by-play man on WGN radio, from 1965–86—one of the longest-tenured men in that role. Previously he'd shared the TV booth on WGN-TV with Jack Brickhouse.

In addition to his catchphrase, Lloyd would often ring a cowbell in the broadcast booth to celebrate a Cubs home run.

6. Former MLB pitcher Jim Deshaies, currently the Cubs' TV analyst, set the MLB record for consecutive strikeouts to begin a game on September 23, 1986, against the Los Angeles Dodgers. Deshaies, then pitching for the Houston Astros, threw a complete-game shutout and held the Dodgers to two hits. Despite the eight Ks to begin the game, Deshaies struck out only two other Dodgers the rest of that game.

Deshaies became a TV analyst with the Astros in 1997 and joined Cubs broadcasts in 2013.

His strikeout record was broken July 11, 2021, when Marlins pitcher Pablo Lopez struck out the first nine Braves he faced.

7. Satellite broadcasting is now common, in fact, it drives much of broadcast television sports, with live feeds sent by orbiting satellites to studios where games are produced and aired by TV channels.

This was all new in 1962, when the first broadcast satellite, Telstar, was sent into Earth orbit.

On July 23, 1962, a couple of minutes of a Cubs game against the Phillies at Wrigley Field were included in a live broadcast from various locations all around the globe. Two Phillies at-bats were shown. One resulted in a fly ball to right, the other a base hit.

Fifteen years later, *Chicago Tribune* columnist Peter Reich revealed that both of those hit balls were somewhat orchestrated by plate umpire Tony Venzon. Venzon had talked about the intercontinental telecast with Jack Brickhouse before the game and apparently decided to take matters into his own hands.

After the game, Brickhouse told Venzon, "We sure were lucky that both of those batters decided to swing when we were on Telstar." Venzon replied, "Lucky, hell! That was my doing. I told them each when they came up to bat, 'Fella, you'd better swing at anything this guy throws, because if it's within three feet of the plate, I'm gonna call it a strike!' I mean, I wasn't gonna let baseball look dull and uninteresting to people in Europe who'd never seen a game before, was I?"

8. Milo Hamilton had been brought on board by WGN-TV in 1981 to join Jack Brickhouse, with the understanding that Brickhouse would retire after the '81 season and Hamilton would succeed him.

Hamilton had previously broadcast Cubs games on WIND radio for three years in the 1950s, then did White Sox and Braves games before returning to Chicago. But when the White Sox dumped Harry Caray after 1981 following the team's sale to Jerry Reinsdorf's group, new Cubs owners the Tribune Company decided to capitalize on Caray's popularity and hire him.

Hamilton and Caray shared the booth, rather uneasily, until Hamilton left after 1984. Hamilton had previously, he felt, been aced out of a job in St. Louis in the 1950s by Caray and didn't care to work with him. Eventually Hamilton moved on to a broadcast job with the Astros and spent 28 seasons there, eventually receiving the Frick Award for broadcast excellence from the Hall of Fame.

9. Here are the eight no-hitters broadcast by WGN-TV:

- May 12, 1955: Sam Jones, Cubs over Pirates
- May 15, 1960: Don Cardwell, Cubs over Cardinals
- August 19, 1965: Jim Maloney, Reds over Cubs
- August 19, 1969: Ken Holtzman, Cubs over Braves
- June 3, 1971: Ken Holtzman, Cubs over Reds
- April 16, 1972: Burt Hooton, Cubs over Phillies
- September 2, 1972: Milt Pappas, Cubs over Padres
- September 15, 2008: Carlos Zambrano, Cubs over Astros

10. Bob Elson and Red Barber. On October 5, 1938, the day of Game One of that year's World Series, the *Chicago Tribune* reported that Elson would do play by play over WGN, while Red Barber would broadcast World Series reports on WMAQ.

11. September 27, 1981, was the Cubs' final home date, the last of a miserable year in which they'd wind up with a 38–65 record in the strike-shortened year.

On that afternoon in 1981, the Cubs would win their final home game, a 14–0 blowout of the Phillies. They led the game 13–0 after five innings, which prompted the Phillies to empty their bench and play substitutes.

One of those players was a skinny kid who'd just turned 22. Phillies manager Dallas Green, soon to become Cubs GM, put the kid at shortstop.

He came to bat in the eighth inning and looped a single to right, his first MLB hit. Cubs broadcaster Jack Brickhouse, doing his final home game, was engrossed in telling a story and barely noted this hit.

And that's how the first hit of future Cub and future Hall of Famer Ryne Sandberg was registered.

12. Jack Quinlan and Lou Boudreau, who shared the Cubs WGN radio booth from 1958–64, often read commercials live on the air. One of them was from a local department store called Wieboldt's, which was having a sale on women's lingerie.

When they got to the place in the script that required them to read, "Wieboldt's has ladies underwear half off," they could not stop laughing. This happened on more than one occasion.

It was a different time.

13. Steve Stone and Len Kasper both broadcast Cubs games for many years, and also later went to call White Sox games.

Stone was a Cubs broadcaster from 1983–2004, and departed

the Cubs under difficult circumstances. Some Cubs players had begun to criticize Stone's honesty on broadcasts and he didn't feel he could continue. Stone became a White Sox broadcaster full time in 2009 and remains there today.

Kasper was the Cubs' TV announcer from 2005–20 and departed Marquee Sports Network after the '20 season to do White Sox radio broadcasts, saying he'd always wanted to call a World Series and as a local TV broadcaster couldn't do that. The Sox were a contending team at the time and Kasper hoped he could do that soon. Obviously that hasn't worked out the way he had hoped.

14. Bob Scheffing managed the Cubs in 1958 and 1959 and thanks in part to Ernie Banks's two MVP seasons, the Cubs contended for a while and won 70-plus games both years, just the second and third time they had done that since 1947.

Inexplicably, team owner P. K. Wrigley fired Scheffing and replaced him with former Cubs star and manager Charlie Grimm, who had previously managed the Cubs to three pennants, but hadn't been with the team since 1949.

Grimm lasted 17 games, going 6–11, before Wrigley decided to do a unique swap—sending Grimm to the WGN radio booth and having analyst Lou Boudreau manage the team.

It wasn't that bad an idea. Boudreau had previously managed nine years in Cleveland and three in Boston, winning a World Series in 1948. But the 1960 Cubs were a terrible team, losing 94 games. Boudreau went back to radio and Grimm was moved into a senior advisory position in the Cubs front office.

15. Jack Quinlan, a native of Peoria, Illinois, began calling Cubs games on WIND radio in 1955, when he was just 28 years old. A rising star in the broadcast industry, he moved along with the team to WGN in 1957, and became popular among Cubs fans.

He won several broadcasting awards and was tapped by NBC radio to call the 1960 World Series.

Quinlan was an avid golfer and had left a golf outing in Arizona during spring training in 1965 when he died in an auto accident. He was just 38 years old.

16. Ron Santo was one of the more popular Cubs of his time. He was also somewhat controversial, wearing his heart on his sleeve, and when he was traded to the White Sox in 1973 not many Cubs fans lamented his departure.

Time has a way of healing these wounds, and Santo returned to the Cubs as a radio analyst in 1990.

Eight years later he was in Milwaukee with play-by-play man Pat Hughes when the Cubs needed just one out to defeat the Brewers, leading 7–5 in the ninth, a key game in a playoff race. The bases were loaded and Geoff Jenkins lifted a lazy fly ball to Brant Brown in left field.

Brown dropped the ball and all three Brewers runners scored and the Cubs lost. Santo's plaintive scream of "Oh, no! No!" is part of Cubs lore.

Santo, visiting the clubhouse after the game, was inconsolable. Cubs manager Jim Riggleman had to give Santo comfort and a pep talk, according to Hughes, "perhaps the first time a manager ever consoled a broadcaster."

The Cubs recovered from the tough loss and won the NL wild card that year anyway.

17. Ron Santo was also part of this bit of Cubs lore, a story Pat Hughes loved to tell.

Santo wore a hairpiece. It was never really mentioned much, just an accepted part of who he was. In early April 2003, the Cubs were in New York to play the Mets, and on a chilly day overhead heaters were at work in the broadcast booth.

Hughes and Santo stood for the national anthem and Hughes later said he heard something "sizzling like bacon." It was Santo's toupee on fire. Hughes poured some water on it and put the fire out.

Hughes loved to tell the story. "He said, 'How does it look?' I lied and said, 'It doesn't look that bad.' It actually looked like a professional golfer had taken a pitching wedge and hit one off his head."

18. Rogers Hornsby, who played for the Cubs from 1929–32 and also managed the team in '32, was hired to be a TV broadcaster for the Cubs on WENR-TV in 1949, seven years after he was elected to the National Baseball Hall of Fame. While no film of Hornsby broadcasting games survives, reports were that he wasn't very good at it and he left broadcasting after that year.

In 1958, Hornsby returned to the Cubs as a coach. In spring training in 1959, he was addressing a group of Cubs prospects and criticizing nearly every one of them. He stopped and pointed at one and said, "You could play in the big leagues right now," and said, "So could you," to another.

Those two players were Billy Williams and Ron Santo. Hornsby could be an irascible sort, but he knew baseball talent when he saw it.

19. Chuck Connors played various roles in TV and film for several decades, becoming best known for his starring role in TV's *The Rifleman* from 1958–63. Before that, though, he played in the majors for two seasons—one at-bat for the Dodgers in 1949 and 66 games for the Cubs in 1951. In his Cubs season, Connors batted .239/.282/.303 with two home runs.

It was in part because of his connection to the Cubs organization that Connors got his chance in Hollywood. At the time, the Triple-A Los Angeles Angels were the Cubs' top affiliate, and Connors played there in 1951 and 1952. According to his SABR biography, Connors got a call from MGM casting director Bill Grady, a big Angels fan, asking Connors to test for a role in the movie *Pat and Mike*, a film starring Spencer Tracy and Katharine Hepburn. Connors got the part playing a police captain and was paid $500 for just a few hours of work. Connors was quoted in a *Sporting News* article in 1966: "I said right then, this is my racket. Playing with Tracy and Hepburn, I was in the big leagues much faster than I arrived there in baseball."

20. Peter Marshall was the longtime genial host of the TV game show *Hollywood Squares.*

But did you know that was just a stage name? Marshall's real name was Ralph Pierre LaCock. (I think you can see why he adopted that stage name.)

If that name rings a bell to you as a Cubs fan, it should. His son, Ralph Pierre LaCock Jr., better known as Pete LaCock, was the Cubs' first-round pick in the January phase of the 1970 draft and played parts of five seasons for the Cubs from 1972–76, as well as four seasons for the Royals. With Kansas City, LaCock had some success and played for them in the 1980 World Series.

LaCock was also a great storyteller. He hit a grand slam off Bob Gibson in Gibson's final MLB game in 1975, the last hit anyone got off Gibson. Years later, the two faced each other in an Old Timers' Game. Gibson hit LaCock with a pitch and according to longtime baseball writer Joe Posnanski, yelled, "I've been waiting YEARS to do that!"

21. Before he became a famous TV broadcaster, both for baseball and hosting game shows, Joe Garagiola had been best known for being Yogi Berra's best friend. The two had grown up in the Italian "Hill" neighborhood in St. Louis and both signed MLB contracts. Berra, of course, went on to a Hall of Fame career.

Garagiola, meanwhile, played nine MLB seasons and batted

just .257/.354/.385 with 42 home runs in 676 games, mostly as a backup catcher. He played for the Cardinals, Pirates, Giants, and parts of two years with the Cubs in 1953 and 1954.

Among his broadcasting highlights, apart from calling baseball games including three World Series, were as the host of *The Today Show*, a guest host for Johnny Carson on *The Tonight Show*, and hosting several game shows: *He Said, She Said*, *Joe Garagiola's Memory Game*, *Sale of the Century*, *To Tell the Truth*, and *Strike It Rich*.

22. Ernie Banks had a varied career off the field. Back in Banks's time, most players had to take offseason jobs to make extra money. Banks sold cars for a while and actually ran for alderman of Chicago's Eighth Ward in 1963. Despite his popularity, he got just 18 percent of the vote.

Around the time when his career was winding up in 1971, WGN-TV tried Banks as a substitute sportscaster. He seemed ill at ease on the air and this gig didn't last long. This writer, though, remembers one particular highlight he was narrating, saying that after a couple of runners got on base, "I came up." Banks did get a hit, driving in a run, in that long-ago game.

23. When Leo Durocher was fired as Giants manager after 1955, he went into television work, becoming a commentator on NBC's baseball coverage and also hosting the network's *The NBC Comedy Hour* and *Jackpot Bowling*.

Durocher went back into baseball with the Dodgers as a coach when they moved to Los Angeles and worked his TV connections into some roles on various TV shows. Perhaps the most memorable of those was an episode of the sitcom *Mister Ed*, featuring the famous "talking" horse. In the episode "Mr. Durocher meets Mr. Ed," after giving advice to the Dodgers, Mister Ed eventually hits a ball off Sandy Koufax and runs around the bases for an inside-the-park home run.

Durocher, of course, eventually managed the Cubs from 1967–72, leading them to their best years since the 1940s, but short of a pennant or World Series. That was in part because Durocher overworked his regulars and didn't have much of a bench.

24. David Ross had quite the varied baseball career. He was a catcher for seven different teams: Braves, Reds, Dodgers, Red Sox, Pirates, Padres, and for two memorable seasons with the Cubs, winning a World Series ring in 2016 and hitting a home run in Game Seven, his final MLB game.

When Theo Epstein's Red Sox acquired Ross in late 2008, he and the coaching staff were impressed by Ross's knowledge of the game in team meetings. It's clear that Epstein remembered that when he acquired Ross, as the Cubs brought him on as a special assistant in the front office after he retired as a player.

During this "special assistant" time, Ross did some work calling games on ESPN, and also made a memorable set of appearances on the TV show *Dancing with the Stars* in 2017. Despite having little or no dance experience when he began this run, Ross and his partner, Lindsay Arnold, made the *DWTS* finals before finishing second.

Ross served as Cubs manager from 2020–23 and won a division title in the first of those seasons, which was shortened by the pandemic. He also had the team in contention for a wildcard spot in September 2023, but the team collapsed down the stretch.

TRUE OR FALSE

QUESTIONS

Each player below played for the Cubs—true or false?

1. Barry Bonds, all-time leader in career home runs.
   Answer on page 143.

2. Lou Boudreau, Hall of Fame shortstop and 1948 American League MVP with Cleveland.
   Answer on page 143.

3. Lew Burdette, pitcher who starred for the Braves in the 1950s.
   Answer on page 143.

4. Smoky Burgess, catcher who for many years held the MLB record for most pinch hits in a career.
   Answer on page 143.

5. Smoky Joe Wood, pitcher who was 117–57 with a 2.03 ERA in 11 seasons, including 34–5 in 1912.
   Answer on page 143.

6. Gary Carter, Hall of Fame catcher.
Answer on page 143.

7. Joe Carter, outfielder who hit a walk-off home run for the Blue Jays to end the 1993 World Series.
Answer on page 143.

8. Rico Carty, outfielder and 1970 National League batting champion with the Braves.
Answer on page 143.

9. Mort Cooper, pitcher who won 65 games for the Cardinals from 1942–44 and National League MVP in 1942.
Answer on page 143.

10. Walker Cooper, Mort's brother; catcher and eight-time All-Star.
Answer on page 143.

11. Chili Davis, outfielder and three-time All-Star.
Answer on page 143.

12. Tommy Davis, National League batting champion with the Dodgers in 1962 and 1963.
Answer on page 143.

13. Willie Davis, outfielder who won three Gold Gloves as a Dodger.
Answer on page 143.

14. Jimmie Foxx, Hall of Fame slugging outfielder.
Answer on page 143.

15. Nellie Fox, Hall of Fame second baseman and 1959 American League MVP with the White Sox.
Answer on page 144.

16. Goose Gossage, Hall of Fame reliever.
Answer on page 144.

17. Goose Goslin, Hall of Fame outfielder and 1928 American League batting champion with the Senators.
Answer on page 144.

18. Ellis Kinder, pitcher who was 102–71 in 12 seasons, including 23–6 for the Red Sox in 1949.
Answer on page 144.

19. Ralph Kiner, Hall of Fame slugger.
Answer on page 144.

20. Harvey Haddix, pitcher who was 136–113 in 14 seasons and pitched 12 perfect innings for the Pirates in a 1959 game.
Answer on page 144.

21. Harvey Kuenn, outfielder who won the American League batting title in 1959 and led the AL in hits four times.
Answer on page 144.

22. Barry Larkin, Hall of Fame shortstop.
Answer on page 144.

23. Don Larsen, author of the celebrated perfect game for the Yankees in the 1956 World Series.
Answer on page 144.

24. Mickey Owen, four-time All-Star as catcher for the Dodgers from 1941–44.
Answer on page 144.

25. Mickey Vernon, first baseman, seven-time All-Star, and two-time American League batting champion with the Senators.
Answer on page 144.

26. Rafael Furcal, shortstop, three-time All-Star, and National League Rookie of the Year with the Braves in 2000.
Answer on page 144.

27. Rafael Palmeiro, first baseman who hit 569 home runs in 20-year career.
Answer on page 144.

28. Robin Roberts, Hall of Fame pitcher.
Answer on page 144.

29. Robin Yount, Hall of Fame shortstop and center fielder.
Answer on page 144.

30. Art Shamsky, outfielder who excelled as a pinch-hitter and was a member of the 1969 "Miracle Mets."
Answer on page 144.

31. Bobby Shantz, pitcher who went 24–7 for the Athletics in 1952 and was voted the American League MVP.
Answer on page 144.

32. Frank Thomas, first baseman, Hall of Famer, and two-time American League MVP with the White Sox.
Answer on page 144.

33. Bobby Thomson, who hit the famous "Shot Heard 'Round the World" to win the pennant for the Giants in 1951.
Answer on page 144.

34. Johnny Vander Meer, who pitched back-to-back no-hitters for the Reds.
Answer on page 144.

35. John Vander Wal, outfielder and first baseman with eight teams in 14 seasons.
Answer on page 144.

36. Hoyt Wilhelm, Hall of Fame pitcher.
Answer on page 144.

37. Waite Hoyt, Hall of Fame pitcher.
Answer on page 144.

TRUE OR FALSE

ANSWERS

1. False; his father, Bobby Bonds, played 45 games for the Cubs in 1981.

2. False; he managed the Cubs but never played for them.

3. True.

4. True.

5. False.

6. False.

7. True.

8. True.

9. True.

10. True.

11. False.

12. True. Davis played 11 games for the Cubs in 1970, was released, then signed again with the Cubs and played 15 games in 1972.

13. False.

14. True.

15. False.

16. True.

17. False.

18. False.

19. True.

20. False.

21. True.

22. False.

23. True.

24. True.

25. False.

26. False.

27. True.

28. True.

29. False.

30. True.

31. True.

32. False. Frank Thomas, outfielder, played 155 of his 1,766 career games as a Cub, in 1960–61 and 1966.

33. True.

34. True.

35. False.

36. True.

37. False.

MISCELLANEOUS

QUESTIONS

1. Johnny Evers was part of the famed Tinker-to-Evers-to-Chance double-play combination, and was elected to the Hall of Fame in 1946. How is his last name pronounced?
   Answer on page 147.

2. Which Cub, through 2025, had hit the team's first home run of the season more often than any other?
   Answer on page 147.

3. Who pinch-hit the most times of any Cub?
   Answer on page 147.

4. Who had the most pinch hits of any Cub?
   Answer on page 147.

5. Who hit the most home runs as a Cubs pinch-hitter?
   Answer on page 147.

6. Which Cubs pitcher pinch-hit the most times?
   Answer on page 147.

7. Six different Cubs had at least five hits in game four different times. How many can you name?
Answer on page 147.

8. Eighty-six Cubs have had at least five hits in a game once. How many have done it multiple times?
Answer on page 148.

9. From 1876–2025, the Cubs used 2,277 players. How many got a hit in their first game with the team?
Answer on page 148.

10. At the end of 1907, the Cubs were 584 games above .500 in regular-season games. How many games above .500 were they at the end of 2025?
Answer on page 148.

11. In what city outside Chicago have the Cubs won more regular-season games than in any other?
Answer on page 148.

MISCELLANEOUS

ANSWERS

1. Many people who see the spelling Evers pronounce the name EH-vers. However, during his lifetime, his friends and family always said it as EE-vers.

2. Frank Schulte, five times, from 1907-09, 1911, and 1913. Three have done it four times: Ernie Banks (1956, 1959, 1962, and 1969), Mark Grace (1992, 1996, 1997, and 1999), and Ian Happ (2018, 2020, 2023, and 2025).

3. Phil Cavarretta, 228 times, four more than Bob Will.

4. Dwight Smith had 50 pinch-hits, four more than Larry Biittner, Phil Cavarretta, and Bob Will.

5. Glenallen Hill had nine pinch home runs. Thad Bosley and Kevin Roberson hit six; Ernie Banks, Ian Happ, and Patrick Wisdom had five pinch long balls.

6. Claude Hendrix pinch-hit 35 times, five more than Carlos Zambrano. None of the other 77 pitchers who pinch-hit did it more than 17 times.

7. Phil Cavarretta, Frank Demaree, Stan Hack, Don Kessinger, Derrek Lee, and Billy Williams.

8. Twenty-eight, of whom nineteen did it exactly twice.

9. 499, so the next to do this will make it an even 500!

10. 582. That means the Cubs had just two more losses than wins over the past 118 seasons.

11. The Cubs have 596 wins in Pittsburgh. They have won 576 in Philadelphia, 566 in St. Louis, and 553 in Cincinnati.

Acknowledgments

First, this book would not have happened if not for Jason Katzman at Skyhorse. While I was pitching a different book idea to him, he asked me if I'd be interested in putting together this one instead, to which I said, "Sure!"

And now you know a bit of how these things come together.

Ken Samelson, who also assisted with my books "Chicago Cubs Firsts" and "A Season For The Ages," also gave editing help on this project and this book would not have been completed without his help.. Thanks also to Jesse McHugh and Kirsten Dalley of Skyhorse for their assistance with this project.

My greatest thanks go to my friends Mike Bojanowski and John Wilheim. They were of great help in assisting with creating the questions, supplying some answers and giving general support to this book project. Their knowledge of Cubs and Wrigley Field history, as always, is unparalleled.

As ever, I am grateful to have been a colleague of the great baseball writer Rob Neyer, whose patient guidance made me a better writer.

Thanks to the Chicago Cubs and their players, coaches, managers, executives, and broadcasters for always creating fascinating moments that are shared with you in this book. May they continue to do so forever.

Lastly and as always, to my life partner Miriam Romain, who shares Cubs baseball and everything else with me every single day, and who was helpful in reading over parts of "The Incredible Chicago Cubs Trivia Book." To you and me always.